ONLY IN NEW YORK

ONLY IN NEW YORK

AN EXPLORATION OF THE WORLD'S MOST FASCINATING, FRUSTRATING, AND IRREPRESSIBLE CITY

SAM ROBERTS

Empire State Editions

An imprint of Fordham University Press

New York   2019

Original edition published 2009 by St. Martin's Press. Fordham University Press
edition published 2019.

Many of the pieces in this book first appeared in a different form as podcasts
available through the *New York Times* website, and to the extent that they are
reprinted here, they are reprinted with permission.

Fordham University Press has no responsibility for the persistence or accu-
racy of URLs for external or third-party Internet websites referred to in this
publication and does not guarantee that any content on such websites is, or will
remain, accurate or appropriate.

Fordham University Press also publishes its books in a variety of electronic
formats. Some content that appears in print may not be available in electronic
books.

Visit us online:
www.empirestateeditions.com
www.fordhampress.com

Library of Congress Control Number: 2018952969

Printed in the United States of America

21 20 19 5 4 3 2 1

Revised edition

to my brothers,
Barry Josephson and Tom McDonald

Contents

New Yorkers

History Lessons

Foreword

The journalistic work of Sam Roberts over the past four decades has always been of a very high order indeed, so it is no surprise that the essays in this collection offer many pleasures. It doesn't matter that they originated as podcasts for the website of the *New York Times*. We all know that the delivery systems of journalism are changing by the week. But they are written by a splendid newspaperman, a New Yorker born and bred, and above all a man of high intelligence, modesty, irony, and wit.

In almost every essay, he provokes the responses of that reader most hoped for by any columnist. First, "I didn't *know* that." Second, "I never *thought* about it that way." When a columnist receives both reactions, he or she knows that the result was a double with men on base.

So here we discover that L. Frank Baum, author of *The Wonderful Wizard of Oz*, was in fact a New Yorker, a discovery that would have delighted my Irish immigrant mother. When I was five, on my first walk across the Brooklyn Bridge, my mother answered my astounded question about the Manhattan skyline by saying it was ... Oz. It was for me, and so it was, and is, for Sam Roberts, another child of Brooklyn. Not many of us knew that Zane Grey was a Manhattan dentist, born in the Bronx, before discovering gold in the mythic purple sage of the American West. And in one essay here Sam reminds us that Henry James grew up in a very different New York, on the site of a huge loft building where the Triangle Shirtwaist fire took place in 1911, and that it's now occupied by New York University.

In short, Sam often penetrates the many layers of New York, the palimpsests of our contemporary existence, and thus helps us see what is present but not visible. He has clearly read much New York history, knowing full well that in a city as complicated, shifting, and unknowable as New York, reading history is also a form of reporting. It can answer the sort of questions that must have been uttered in ancient Mesopotamia: *Who are we? Why are we here? Where are we going?* We live in the present, of course, and imagine the future, but at the same time we are shaped by the collective past. Certain New York fundamentals do not shift: the harbor, the rivers, the climate, the traditions (going back to the Dutch) of tolerance, along with our recurring fantasies of apocalypse and our permanent gifts for bitching. All are in this collection, driven by Sam's inexhaustible curiosity and sense of discovery.

Like most New Yorkers, he has no illusions about making the city into a utopia. He knows, as we all do, that politicians can't solve all problems; at best, they can manage them. Most New Yorkers accept that reality with a kind of healthy fatalism, as if living by Antonio Gramsci's mantra "optimism of the well, pessimism of the intelligence."

But Sam Roberts is also a child of Brownsville, whose spawn has ranged from Alfred Kazin to Willie Randolph, and included Jewish prizefighters, Jewish gangsters, and Jewish kids who dreamed of being artists, writers, lawyers, and cops. Sam was born in 1947, when many Brownsville residents still believed in the utopian promises of socialism (they had even elected socialists to the City Council). The Depression and the Second World War had cut into all of them what the historian Caroline Bird once called "the invisible scar." A minority even embraced the iron-headed variety of communism that bowed to Joseph Stalin, in the years before his dreadful crimes had been fully exposed. By the time Sam was a teenager, disillusion had set in, and his generation understood that ideology was not thinking; it was a substitute for thought.

In his two pieces about the case of Julius and Ethel Rosenberg, he deals with the way Stalinist utopianism could lead to betrayal and death. In 2001, his book about the Rosenberg case was published. The book drew upon the first interviews with David Greenglass, the brother of Ethel Rosenberg. In its pages, Greenglass was filled with anguish, some regret, the soul-killing duty of making powerful moral choices. Sam, in these columns and in his book, approached the case with a reporter's objectivity. He is neither prosecutor nor counsel for the defense. He is a reporter. The results were clear. Sam had uncovered something new about an ancient, almost mythic case, and that myth would have to be examined again, even by those who defended it with so much abiding, often enraged passion. Few writers ever accomplish so much.

But the concern about the story of the Rosenbergs is not totally abstract. It was also pushed by a dim memory from Sam's Brooklyn youth. He was among the thousands who observed the passing of the funeral cortège after the Rosenbergs were executed in 1953. The cars moved through Brownsville on the way to the cemetery in Pinelawn, on Long Island. The day before, Sam Roberts turned six. All of us have images from that age that will be with us until we die.

Other essays have roots in Sam's Brooklyn childhood. The moments are not always as chilling as a funeral. He passes a bakery and remembers the aroma of the bakery near Ebbets Field, during his first visits to the vanished ballpark. (I came from a different part of Brooklyn but remember the same bakery.) He knows that in 1947, the year of his own birth, Jack Roosevelt Robinson first walked on the sweet grass of Ebbets Field and, in effect, started the modern civil rights movement that would culminate decades later in the election of Barack Obama. By the time Sam was ten, the Dodgers were gone and Robinson had retired, and both of them had been hammered into the palimpsest.

He sees a 2007 report about the closing of five Brooklyn high schools. One of them, Samuel J. Tilden, was where Sam spent what he calls here his "wonder years." At Tilden, he made his first tentative steps toward becoming a newspaperman. He went on to Cornell University and worked for the school paper and as a stringer for the *New York Times*, the Associated Press, and *Time*. He graduated in 1968 and went to work as a reporter for the *New York Daily News*.

He could not have imagined then what was to come: fifteen years as a reporter and editor at the *Daily News* (where I worked with him as a columnist in the 1970s) and then, after 1983, a luminous career at the *New York Times* as a reporter and editor that continues to this day. In 1968, that ferocious and terrible year for news, he could not have imagined what was coming. Nobody could. Who could have predicted the disappearance of the hammering chorus of manual typewriters on the brink of a collective deadline? Or city rooms where nobody could smoke? Or city rooms located far from printing plants? Or cable television? Or iPhones and other mobile devices? The Internet was beyond our imaginations at the newspapers where we worked. Sam Roberts became one of those fortunate journalists who witnessed, and was part of, a great journalistic and cultural transition. It was no accident that when cable television arrived, he became the face of the *New York Times* on NY1 and CUNY-TV. And in 1968, nobody in any city room on the planet could have imagined podcasts.

But here he is, Sam Roberts, full of honors, yet still true to his beginnings, with New York encoded in his DNA, telling us things that are new, forcing us to think of past and present in fresh ways. And suggesting that possibilities of the future. For me, it has been a pleasure to read him and learn from him and to share the pleasure of his company.

Pete Hamill

Preface to the Fordham University Press Edition

With New York City poised to celebrate its 400th birthday, you'd be amazed at the difference made during the last decade alone. Since the first edition of *Only in New York* was published, New York's singularity has been even more pronounced even as the city's historic diversity became more commonplace everywhere.

New York still boasts the nation's largest urban population, the tallest skyscraper in the Western hemisphere, the most billionaires, the highest number of homeless people, the biggest disparities in income, the greatest degree of residential segregation and waste paper as its chief export.

Unlike many other older cities in America, New York is also growing again. Since 2010, the number of New Yorkers counted each year set new records, so much so that when the 2020 census is completed, the official population will probably surpass 8.6 million. Even the Bronx, a late-twentieth-century synonym for hopelessness, is being revived as an influx of immigrants and creative and professional newcomers priced out of booming neighborhoods in Manhattan and Brooklyn boosted the number of residents to a historic high.

Two decades after Spike Lee's 1994 film *Crooklyn* captured a black ghetto struggling in the 1970s, the movie *Brooklyn*, adapted from Colm Tóibín's novel, evoked the promise of the early 1950s (for whites) while implicitly lionizing the latest renaissance of a borough that periodically numbers royalty among its residents these days (the *Queen Mary 2* now docks there). In Queens, half the population comes from other counties, rivaling only Miami-Dade in Florida among large counties in their proportion of residents born abroad. In part, because of the recession, for a time more people moved to the city than left, reversing a trend that had prevailed for decades and achieving a racial equilibrium that contrasted with earlier fears of white flight.

While felony rates have zigzagged in other cities, recorded crime in New York has plunged to levels unseen since at least the 1950s (when the public's chief complaint was quaintly described as juvenile delinquency).

More than a century has elapsed since the city expanded beyond its borders by annexing appreciable plots of land. Instead, it keeps recycling itself, generating nonstop nostalgia while providing imaginative new vistas. Elaine's and the Four Seasons restaurants closed. The Waldorf Astoria was shuttered for renovations (there's always Airbnb.com now, though few apartments compare with the Waldorf's presidential suite).

The Second Avenue subway finally opened (at least a three-stop spur did). So did the High Line on a derelict elevated railroad track and the defiantly tall World Trade Center that replaced the Twin Towers. Construction boomed in Midtown West with a giant residential and commercial development called Hudson Yards. Bold high-rise waterfront housing belatedly blossomed to create entire new communities in Williamsburg and Long Island City. The skyline was festooned with twinkling turrets and cornices (some shamelessly self-promotional) like candles on a cake, as well as needle-thin Manhattan condo skyscrapers scooped up at bloated prices by captains of industry and foreign princes (whose affection for the city was belied by their crepuscular windows after dusk, which peg the owners as absentee landlords).

The "city of the Manhattoes," as Herman Melville called it, is no longer "belted round by wharves" that disconnected its insular residents from the sea. New York has rediscovered its waterfront. But the city's remarkable resiliency after the 9/11 terrorist attack was tested again in 2012 by its shocking vulnerability during Hurricane Sandy. The tidal estuaries that had transformed a sleepy seventeenth-century Dutch trading post into America's premier port surged unchallenged to temporarily reclaim the low-lying landfill that fringed the shifting shoreline's manmade bulkheads.

Waterborne transportation proliferated both for commuters and for junketeers (among the biggest sightseeing bargains is still the free Staten Island ferry). So did new, unparalleled vistas from the visionary Brooklyn Bridge Park and Governors Island and other new destinations, including the red-brick retro Citi Field, the latest incarnation of Yankee Stadium, the Whitney Museum of Art downtown, The Met Breuer, and, on Roosevelt Island, a sleek Cornell University campus and an arcadian sanctuary called Four Freedoms Park, which ennobles the island's namesake.

Some already existing places were spruced up. Others were also relabeled. Near the southern tip of Manhattan, the city's collective memory was tardily rekindled when a tiny plot was designated as Evacuation Day Plaza to commemorate the departure of British troops after the American Revolution. Whether the new names will be widely embraced is debatable, though. New Yorkers of a certain age still refer to 30 Rockefeller Plaza as the RCA Building—even though it was rechristened to honor GE and later Comcast. And be wary of directing cab drivers to the newly named Robert F. Kennedy Bridge, the Hugh L. Carey Tunnel, or the Ed Koch Bridge (instead of the Triborough Bridge, the Brooklyn-Battery Tunnel and the Queensboro–59th Street Bridge, respectively). While cashless tolling was implemented on some bridges, transportation officials mulled imposing congestion-pricing fees for motorists who used other spans to enter Manhattan.

For that matter, many yellow taxis have themselves been supplanted by Uber and Lyft drivers and by lime-green cabs, which now serve Upper Manhattan and the other four boroughs (all of which have contributed to ending the monopoly that propped up the prices of taxi medallions, which plummeted in value from as much as $1.3 million each as recently as 2013 to less than $250,000 in 2017). Elongated buses and bicycles now claim their own lanes on New York streets (further constricted by Citi-Bike stands). Countdown clocks may not speed mass transit but are at least taking the guesswork out of trainspotting by subway riders underground and of peering down the block from hundreds of long-overdue bus shelters. Mass transit riders are still reading, but largely on their personal digital devices, not newspapers. Folding the *Times* lengthwise to accommodate fellow passengers on crowded subway trains is fast becoming a lost art.

In 2013, New Yorkers elected a liberal mayor, Bill de Blasio, who was surprisingly good at proving that a progressive politician could also administer the cumbersome municipal bureaucracy (in good times, anyway). Four years later, he became the first Democratic mayor to win a second term since 1985. In 2016, the nation's voters sent a New Yorker to the White House for the first time since 1944 (unless you count Dwight Eisenhower, who was president of Columbia University, or Richard M. Nixon, who lived on Fifth Avenue—in the same building as Nelson A. Rockefeller—before he was elected in 1968). That 1944 race was also the last time two New Yorkers (Franklin D. Roosevelt and Thomas E. Dewey) squared off as major-party nominees. Chuck Schumer was elected the first Senate minority leader from New York. (After the 2020 census, though, the state's dwindling congressional delegation is likely to shrink again as the center of gravity of the nation's population shifts West and South.)

Another Cuomo (Andrew, son of Mario) was elected governor in 2009. Since then, same-sex marriage was legalized in New York state and the City Council elected a speaker who is gay. (Gay marchers were also finally welcomed to join the St. Patrick's Day parade.)

All those changes occurred in just the last decade. The breathtaking metamorphosis has provided plenty of grist for the latest version of *Only in New York*. It's also a reminder, as the city enters its fifth century, of something O. Henry said presciently more than a hundred years ago. "New York," he predicted, "will be a great place if they ever finish it."

ONLY IN NEW YORK

Introduction

Here's a sobering thought: I've been covering New York and what makes it tick for more than 10 percent of the city's existence. During five decades, I've been granted the opportunity to plumb the personalities of power brokers, celebrate the city's diversity, get to know some of its zany characters, champion the extraordinarily ordinary people who have made a difference, and ponder some of the more puzzling mysteries about urban America, including questions that people with more serious jobs might never have thought to ask.

I'm lucky enough to have been a lifelong New Yorker in a city where nearly everyone comes from someplace else. And to have been a reporter and editor for newspapers with the biggest circulation in America and with the greatest reputation. I was city editor of the New York *Daily News* during the crazy summer of 1977. Since 1983, I've been a reporter, editor, and columnist for the *New York Times*; the urban affairs correspondent; the author of mini-biographies called obituaries; the anchor for twenty-five years of the *Times*'s regular television program, now on CUNY-TV; and the former writer and voice of a weekly *Times* podcast about things that could happen only in New York. It's called "Only in New York."

Each of these self-contained essays, nearly all of them adapted from those podcasts, offers an idiosyncratic prism on what makes New York unique—insights that may surprise residents and out-of-towners alike. Just how big is the Big Apple? Why doesn't the renovated Plaza hotel, where apartments start at $2 million, have window screens? Why wasn't the crosstown street grid imposed according to the compass? How did

1

New York inspire the Western novelist Zane Grey? Is it noisier in New York City or in the country, where a puddle in the kitchen was the closest I came to Walden Pond? What makes an Upper East Side restaurant cursed? Do we really need doormen? Who actually runs New York? Why can't you keep roosters in the city? How many months does it take to fix a light bulb? And guess what I saw in the subway.

The podcasts are about people: New Yorkers. Who are they? Why did they come here? Why do they keep complaining but rarely quit the city for someplace else? When I asked readers of the *Times* website, nytimes .com, whether they would ever consider leaving, plenty replied that they were fed up with high taxes imposed by political lowlifes and were already packing—if only they could sell their house or apartment—or they had already fled the city and didn't miss it, or that New York is no longer the city they remember or no place to raise kids—or even a dog—and that to survive you've got to be rich or young. One wrote: "People wear the 'New Yorker' badge with unwarranted honor, a sign of some sort of victory." Some readers sounded downright desperate: Even if they could leave, where would they go?

Which was precisely the point made by so many other New Yorkers who live in the city or who left and can't wait to move back.

"From all the comments on here," one reader wisely remarked, "one would think that 'quality of life' boiled down to disposable income and square footage."

Said another: "It comes down to this: Do you want to live in the greatest city in the U.S.A. or do you want to save $2,000 a year and live in the suburbs of St. Louis? It sure sounds like some of you are disappointed in New York because you never figured out how to live here."

Still another placed the high costs in context: "Yes, everyone knows that living here is expensive, but there's a reason: It simply adds up to demand. It's expensive to be here because so many other people want to be here as well, because the city has so much to offer."

These essays are about a city that too often forgets what its past has to offer and sometimes shortsightedly forgoes its future. New Yorkers are consumed with the present. Yet the chief constant in a city that will celebrate its quadricentennial in 2025 (or 2024, depending on who's counting) is change.

When I joined the *News* full time in 1968, the newsroom resounded with the staccato clatter of manual typewriters. Each evening, underground presses reverberated at least as high as the seventh-floor city room as they disgorged millions of newspapers to a fleet of waiting delivery trucks. Today the *Times*'s newest home can seem eerily quiet. The presses have been moved miles away. The old newsroom's claustrophobia has given way to expanse and transparency. The Metro Desk overlooks a stunning atrium punctuated with white birch trees that are struggling valiantly to acclimate to midtown Manhattan and that evoke the rustic New West more than the rambunctious West Side. (From my own desk I'm lucky to have an earthy vista of Eighth Avenue and the bus terminal.)

The *Times* itself, though, is very much alive. The newspaper is less stenographic, more relevant, and in some ways an even more assuring and indispensable morning touchstone in a nonstop torrent of breaking news and a bottomless pit of bloviation. On the Web, nytimes.com is renewed and enriched continually with vivid graphics, slide shows, video, and audio well beyond the current capacity of tree-grown paper, as we know it, to reproduce.

All stories—whether they are delivered in print or on the Web—still begin with events and people and ideas. Reporting is transformed into words, sometimes fitfully, for history's proverbial first draft. Those words may have been typed on a clunky upright Underwood, written on a contoured ergonomically correct Apple keyboard, translated into characters by voice-recognition software, or spoken into digital recorders. It doesn't matter. What's important is whether they stir the reader or the listener in some way: to laugh, to cry, to pause for a moment, to think, or, even when the topic may at first seem familiar, to recognize, explore, and perhaps embrace a different point of view. What distinguishes this anthology, and demonstrates the resiliency of both the message and the medium, is that it has squared the circle: from the written word to a spoken podcast to transcripts at nytimes.com to a printed book.

Thank you, reader and listener, for partaking of the insights I've gleaned. Covering the city is a forever roller-coaster evolution through some of the worst and best of times, invariably enriched by those weird and wonderful things that could happen only in New York.

Only in New York

The Biggest Apple

The Census Bureau announced recently that no American city is home to more Hawaiian- and Pacific Islander–owned businesses—2,400 of them—than . . . Honolulu. Well, big surprise. But what surprised me was which city is second: New York, with more than 2,300.

With about 8.2 million people in all, New York is a city of superlatives. But just how big is it?

Well, New York has more Latinos than any other city, twice as many Asians as Los Angeles, twice as many blacks as Chicago. More Native Americans live here than in any other city.

It's so big that more people speak Spanish, Urdu, Arabic, Chinese, Japanese, Yiddish . . . and English. It's home to more who identify their heritage as Italian, German, Scottish, Nigerian, or Swiss than any other American city. More who claim Irish ancestry than any other city in the world—including Dublin.

More people born in Pakistan, France, Greece, Israel, Lebanon, Ghana, New Zealand, the Dominican Republic, and almost every other country (except, pretty much, for Cuba and Mexico) live in New York than in any other city in the country.

New York even ranks first in the number of people who describe themselves as having been born at sea (including some who still seem to be at sea).

The city also has more lawyers, doctors, teachers, security guards, construction workers, firefighters, railway workers, and more people who work in arts and entertainment and more people employed in manufacturing.

It doesn't lead in agriculture, although it ranks a pretty respectable tenth nationwide among cities whose residents say their occupation is farming, fishing, or forestry.

New York has more students enrolled in every grade, from kindergarten through graduate school; more who have not graduated from high school and more with doctoral degrees.

The city also ranks first with more people in every age group (including 121,000 who are age eighty-five and older).

New York has more people than any other American city who don't own a car, more who car-pool to work or take public transportation, including taxis and ferries, more who ride their bicycles or walk to work, and more who work at home. San Francisco edges New York, though, in the number who say they commute by motorcycle.

More New Yorkers live in jails, nursing homes, college dorms, mental wards, and religious quarters—like convents—than in any other city.

Now, of course, a few of those numbers might be statistical anomalies, especially since the census relies largely on self-identification. For example, there are undoubtedly a lot of Native Americans in New York, but the total might, in fact, be inflated by some Asian Indians who also consider themselves American and described themselves that way—incorrectly by the government's definition—on the census forms.

In the late nineteenth century, some New Yorkers had the elitist notion that only 400 people in the city really counted. The author O. Henry credited "a wiser man"—the census taker—with what he called a "larger estimate of human interest." O. Henry memorialized them in fiction as *The Four Million*.

Enormous as New York must have seemed then, his 4 million of a century ago have doubled.

New York has more than twice as many people as the nation's second-biggest city, Los Angeles. New York is home to more people than the next four top-ranked cities in population—Chicago, Houston, Philadelphia, and Phoenix—combined.

No group categorized by ancestry or age or birthplace abroad or occupation or degree of education dominates, because, as Theodore Dreiser once wrote, New York "is so preponderantly large."

In every category, each separate New York superlative is subsumed by the biggest superlative of them all: the Eight Million.

June 27, 2006

Since this podcast, the city's population has surpassed a record 8.6 million.

The (How) Big Apple?

Debate persists about why New York is known as the Big Apple. But you'd think by now we'd be able to say precisely how big it is.

Think again.

Recently, I needed to verify New York's exact size for an article I was writing. I started with *The Green Book*, the city's official directory. There, between a meticulous description of the city seal and a calendar of budget deadlines, was the figure: 321.9 square miles.

Frankly, I've always been a little wary about the current edition of *The Green Book* because its cover is bright orange—to commemorate Christo's *Gates*, which graced Central Park in 2005.

So, ever skeptical, I checked further.

The Census Bureau says New York encompasses 303 square miles. The *Encyclopedia Britannica* said 309. The National Geodetic Survey referred me to Wikipedia, which said 322, and to the city's official tourism website, which says 301.

Nothing about New York is static, of course. Every statistic is merely a snapshot of a moving target. And some numbers can suggest false precision.

I remember during the city's fiscal crisis in 1975 covering a meeting between Walter Wriston, the chairman of Citicorp, and Deputy Mayor Jim Cavanagh. Wriston asked what seemed like a relatively straightforward question: Exactly how many people worked for city government? Cavanagh stammered, then finally fished a slip of paper out of his pocket and revealed the number: 397,402.

But an economist working for Wriston noticed that the paper was completely blank.

"That," Wriston later recalled, "was when I knew we were in trouble."

Earlier this year, Mayor Bloomberg vowed to revoke some of the 70,000 or so official parking permits that had been doled out by the city to private vehicles. The mayor kept his commitment—but only after a more thorough inventory found that the actual number of permits was more than 140,000. No wonder there's no place to park.

Which brings us back to the size of the city.

For centuries, its boundaries have been altered by nature and by the hand of man. We lost territory in 1899, when Nassau County was created. And again a century later, when federal courts gave most of Ellis Island to New Jersey.

Meanwhile, thousands of acres were added by landfill, much of it for development in Lower Manhattan and for runways at Kennedy and La Guardia airports.

When I called city officials to reconcile the competing land-area figures, it turned out that the mayor's yen for precision had already prompted planners to recalibrate their own estimate. Instead of the 322 square miles that *The Green Book* had stated definitively for 20 years, geographers discovered that the city really encompasses just under 305 square miles.

Miraculously, Michael Miller, the Planning Department's deputy director of information technology, had resisted the temptation to immediately phone home and inform his wife: "Honey, I shrank the city."

By seventeen square miles, no less! A difference of seventeen square miles may not seem like much, but consider this: That amount of space could accommodate thirteen replicas of Central Park and two dozen countries the size of Monaco. If it were populated at the same density as Manhattan, New York might be home to a million more people. The vacant land would be worth about $1 trillion.

But Miller emphasized that the lower estimate shouldn't make us feel any more dense. He attributed it almost entirely to more precise measuring— not to shoreline erosion or to rising sea levels caused by global warming.

After my call, the Planning Department promptly notified the editors of *The Green Book* just in time to meet the deadline for the 2008 edition. It's due to be published with the more accurate land-area figure. And with the familiar green cover.

May 22, 2008

The latest edition is green again, but it is not as complete as the original and is published in print only sporadically. By 2011, the city had shriveled to 302.6 square miles.

A Streetlight Named Desire

There are 330,000 streetlights in the naked city. This is the story of only one of them. But it vividly illuminates the frustration ordinary New Yorkers sometimes endure and the hurdles Mayor Bloomberg himself faces in improving the city's quality of life—and light.

The streetlight in this story is on the north side of East 96th Street, between Madison and Park. If you can't get a streetlight fixed on the Upper East Side, then where can you?

Yet what began in January 2007 as Martin Daniels's routine complaint to 311, New York's call center for non-emergencies, became a misadventure in *Alice in Wonderland* bureaucracy. It's a turn of events that city officials are still at a loss to fully explain, and it apparently ended only after Public Advocate Betsy Gotbaum intervened.

Daniels is a sixty-six-year-old semi-retired computer programming analyst. Most people might see a burned-out streetlight and look the other way. For Daniels, that would have been out of character. He is one of those confessed New York *nudniks*. Dozens of times a year, he telephones city officials about a smorgasbord of local irritants that are supposed to be fixed sooner rather than later and without the intercession of persistent citizens.

This time, with the streetlight broken after a few days, Daniels could no longer restrain himself. Meanwhile, his wife, a nurse, had to navigate the darkened 96th Street corridor when her shift ended. Fed up, he finally telephoned 311.

Which prompts the proverbial question: How many months does it take to change a light bulb?

In this case, the city admits to at least eight months. Con Ed and Daniels insist that the repairs took fully a year and a day.

Glitches combined to thwart Martin Daniels's attempts to be a good citizen. To begin with, the city's Streetlighting Maintenance Code Sheet lists nearly fifty potential defects. Mechanical complications were compounded by miscommunication. The city switched contractors.

But whether the repair on East 96th Street took twelve months or only eight months may seem beside the point when the city says the average time to fix a defective streetlight has been reduced to just two days—down from nineteen days three years ago. Even if the repair is more complicated and requires Con Ed's intervention, the average last year was under thirteen days, compared with nearly eighty-four days in 2005.

That's assuming only one agency, the Transportation Department, is involved. In Bowling Green Park, in Lower Manhattan, a jurisdictional dispute appears to have delayed the repair of eight decorative light fixtures for four months.

Martin Daniels's charge of his one-man light brigade, as reported in the *Times*, resonated with scores of readers.

Some expressed surprise at how quickly their own complaints have been dealt with by the city—compared with, as one pointed out, the eighteen-month delay in pruning a tree in Bulgaria.

Still others were amazed that anything works at all. A Texan wrote, "Before writing a silly populist story like this, you could have done a little math and figured out that most likely the problem is that there are too many lights, not enough days in the year and not enough people to work on all of them."

One reader described 311 as "a ploy of Orwellian dimensions," adding, "While pretending to be the all-empowering agency that enables us to speak directly to the city, it is in fact a foil that stands between us and the departments within our government with whom we need to communicate."

Readers also wondered why it's taking fully five years to renovate Frederick Douglass Circle, on the northwest corner of Central Park. Why, while some streetlights don't go on at night, do some seem never to go off during the day?

How many light bulbs does it take to drive a lifelong New Yorker out of his Manhattan neighborhood?

After his wife retired, Martin Daniels decided to move south. In this case, about a half-mile south, just six blocks from the mayor's townhouse.

It's a neighborhood where, he figures, public officials are more responsive to citizen-complaint calls.

"I'm not going to give up calling," Daniels told me, "but the number of phone calls will be down."

February 12, 2009

Fighting Words

Fleet Week in New York: The city is teeming with men and women in spiffy uniforms, which means that romantics—gay or straight—who've been raised on old war movies can sidle up to any bar in Midtown and finally get their chance to say, "Buy this sailor a drink."

New York state is credited as the birthplace of Memorial Day.

And more military veterans live here than in any other metropolitan area in the country.

But the number of veterans in New York and the rest of the nation is dwindling.

And New York's rich military history has been largely forgotten.

Truth is, I was reminded of it myself only recently by my wife, who runs the nonprofit National Parks of New York Harbor Conservancy, which just started running a water tour called America's Frontline.

New York is where the first cannonball of the Revolutionary War smashed into the roof of Fraunces Tavern, which still stands in Lower Manhattan.

Where George Washington saved the Continental Army by evacuating it by boat from Brooklyn Heights.

Where the artillery of interlocking harbor forts kept the British from firing even a single shot in the War of 1812.

Where the *Monitor* was clad in iron during the Civil War.

Where the battleship *Maine*—remember the *Maine*?—was launched.

Where German saboteurs touched off the Black Tom explosion of munitions bound for Europe in World War I.

Where a German U-boat surfaced off Coney Island in World War II but was thwarted from entering the harbor by submarine netting.

Where the battleships that began and ended the war in the Pacific—the *Arizona* and the *Missouri*—were built.

And where America was attacked in 2001.

On the military history tour, Lee Gruzen, a writer, recalls her evacuation from Lower Manhattan that morning on a small boat that ferried her to Jersey City.

She recalls, "I felt as if I were reliving a memory of other evacuations in the oddest, most primal way. I've lived on the water my whole life. My ancestors have all lived on the water. And one of my ancestors was with George Washington after the Battle of Brooklyn when the American forces were overrun. And thankfully, they were able to be transported by a whole collection of volunteer vessels to take them from Brooklyn to Manhattan, which, of course, made the whole American Revolution possible and successful."

9/11 inspired stirrings of patriotism and pangs of goodwill toward New York, but how many Americans remember that New Yorkers accounted for a third of Union casualties at Gettysburg and one-sixth of the troops America sent overseas in World War I?

As recently as 1980, the 660,000 civilian veterans in New York City accounted for 12 percent of the adult population. By 2000, the 470,000 remaining veterans made up less than 8 percent. Today the number has declined to fewer than 260,000, or only 4 percent.

Thousands of reservists and National Guard soldiers from the city—including 1,000 or so municipal employees—are on active duty overseas. About 2,500 relatively recent vets are attending City University under the G.I. Bill.

But fully half of the city's veterans are sixty-five or older.

As recently as last year, the city hosted sixteen parades to commemorate Memorial Day. The latest Fleet Week schedule for 2007 lists ten.

Andrew Carroll, who has edited anthologies of letters from veterans, recalls, "To many young people today, World War II is as much ancient history as the Civil War was to the generation who fought in the Second World War. But to the veterans who are now in their seventies, eighties, and nineties, the memories are so raw and so vivid, the war still seems like yesterday."

Many, he says, "expressed to me a fear that war—and not any specific conflict, but warfare itself—was increasingly being romanticized in the popular culture, particularly with video games, movies, television shows, and fashion."

And it's not just about nostalgia, Carroll explained. "With the passing of every veteran," he said, "we lose one more voice to remind us of the harsh realities of warfare and the sacrifices demanded of those who serve, as well as their loved ones on the home front."

November 8, 2007

Go Figure

Okay, I admit it. I was reading the mayor's management report again.

Our reporter Sewell Chan did a great job of covering the 2006 report in the *Times* the other day, but I can't help poring over all 204 pages myself. Don't tune out yet. I'm fascinated—maybe you will be, too—by the statistical nuggets that might not make news stories all by themselves but that say something about what makes New York City unique.

Consider, for example, that the Parks Department planted 9,100 trees last year. Or that the average annual cost of keeping an inmate in the Rikers Island jail complex is more than $66,000—and that, by the way, only one escaped in 2005. Or that 100,000 New Yorkers are diagnosed and living with AIDS. Or that the most complaints to the city's 311 inquiry phone line aren't about landlords or lack of heat, defective streetlights, or even cars that have been towed, but about noise—351,000 of them last year. Or that a pathetic 4 percent or so of branch libraries are open seven days a week.

Ever wonder why the skyline is dotted with cranes—not the flying kind? Or why you're always having to dodge cement mixers, perpetual scaffolding, and all sorts of other obstructions? Not counting all those illegal conversions, the city issued nearly 8,000 building permits for new construction last year and another 8,000 for major renovations.

Take the Staten Island ferry. Please. Since 1898, when Staten Island became part of New York City, and until 1975, the ferry fare was a nickel. Even after it was raised to fifty cents, it was still one of the city's best bargains. In 1997, the fare was scrapped altogether after the MTA switched to free transfers. Mayor Giuliani said all New Yorkers should pay the same to commute. Giuliani just happened to be running for reelection that year.

For Staten Islanders, that meant the bus-to-ferry-to-subway fares, and back again, dropped from $6.50 daily to $3.00. But here's a factoid gleaned from the management report: In 1997, when the fare was abolished, it cost the city $2.40 to carry each passenger. Since then, the city's subsidy has nearly doubled. Today each time a passenger boards the ferry, it costs all New Yorkers collectively $4.50.

Self-interest aside here, if you're listening to a podcast, that may mean you're not a regular newspaper reader. Bad for business. Not just for the people who own newspapers, but for the taxpayers. The city sells the paper it collects to recyclers. Compared with the prior year, the amount of paper collected, including newspapers, fell nearly 5 percent, to 397,000 tons. So did the price. Which means the city made nearly $4 million less than it did the year before.

Talk about liquid assets, here's another insight. Reported crime is lower in New York City than at any time since the 1960s. So are the welfare rolls. And even with the city's population now at a peak, New Yorkers are using less water than in any year since the early 1950s.

The connection among water, welfare, and crime is not entirely co-incidental. Each decline is the result, in part, of government policies.

In New York, municipal water has historically been relatively cheap for consumers. Until residential metering was instituted beginning in the late 1980s, we even were left with the illusion that water (most of it flows freely to the city by gravity) was free. Metering has cut consumption. So has conservation, through incentives to use low-flush toilets, low-flow shower heads, and more efficient washing machines. And forget about leaks in this administration.

Surprisingly perhaps, Emily Lloyd, the city's environmental protection commissioner, says one factor that hasn't made much difference in usage is the proliferation of bottled water. In fact, the city is about to launch a promotional campaign to persuade new immigrants that they're wasting money on the bottled variety because the water here is safe to drink.

"We're going to all this trouble to make the water clean," Lloyd says. "I hope they're drinking it."

September 28, 2006

Park No Cars

Imagine a street sign that cautioned, "Park No Cars," instead of simply saying, "No Parking." Or one that proclaimed, "Trespass Not," instead of "No Trespassing."

Stop and think about that the next time you see one of those forbidding "Post No Bills" warnings stenciled on fences and construction sites or on any other vacant canvas in New York that isn't already covered by posters. Many of the posters were placed there illegally. The more durable ones that now saturate the city are on building walls that landlords themselves have rented to advertisers.

"Post No Bills," of course, isn't the only silly sign.

One of my favorite candidates for most obscure road sign is "Limited Sight Distance." Presumably, it means that because you're going up a hill or around a curve, your visibility is impaired.

One that invariably makes me giggle warns about "Depressed Storm Drains." C'mon. Somebody cheer them up.

Or the one affixed to the back of trucks that says, "Construction Vehicle, Do Not Follow." Why would you?

Public consternation over "Post No Bills" isn't new, of course. It's just one of those quirky urban phenomena that I fixate on during a slow news day.

"The most threatened man in the English-speaking world must be named William Stickers," the *Times*'s columnist William Safire once wrote. "Throughout Great Britain, blank walls and freshly painted fences bear the admonition:'Bill Stickers will be prosecuted.' His accomplice, Bill Posters, has also been widely warned."

The first reference I could find to that admonition in the *New York Times* was published 110 years ago. An editorial remarked on "the legal absurdity that makes it necessary to place this inhibition on every fence, wall or ash can whose owner objects to having his property made into an unremunerative advertising medium."

Early in the twentieth century, rival bill posters would fight to claim blank spaces.

One memorable battle was witnessed by 3,000 New Yorkers in Herald Square, where the old Broadway Tabernacle was being demolished. Crews from competing firms that claimed the franchise to blanket the remaining walls of the structure wielded paste brushes and fists as posters flew. This wasn't the case of three sheets to the wind, but thousands.

Section 145.30 of the New York Penal Code prohibits the unlawful affixing of advertisements to someone else's property.

The charge ranks as a violation. The law is rarely enforced. It's next to impossible, unless you catch someone in the act. In one of those rare cases of someone's being prosecuted for that crime alone, last August a defendant in Manhattan was sentenced to time served—the hours he spent in custody after his arrest.

And what some people denounce as defacement akin to graffiti, others regard as free expression.

In 1991, when Norman Siegel was executive director of the New York Civil Liberties Union, he got the courts to overturn that portion of the law which penalized people whose names appeared on posters illegally affixed to public property. The court said the law hindered the First Amendment.

In a letter to the *Times*, Joan Davidson, the New York arts patron, mused about the inspiring wall posters in Beijing and Shanghai, posters that proclaimed the people's longing for "more readable novels" and for "a social life that is not just meetings." Davidson asked: "Who can foresee what songs the walls of New York might sing?"

"In the name of freedom of expression—and of a livelier streetscape as well," she wrote, "why NOT post bills?"

You'd be hard-pressed to find New York poster men listed by profession in the phone book. Still, politicians, theater owners, and other self-promoters never have trouble reaching them.

My favorite was John Moran.

Moran always made sure he knew where a candidate lived, so he could disproportionately plaster the route between his home and his headquarters with campaign posters.

And then there's the legend often cited as the paradigm of the honest politician.

Moran got the contract to paste up election-eve posters for one candidate in Brooklyn. Then, supposedly he got another contract from the candidate's opponent to tear down those same posters.

He billed both candidates for his work. But did he cynically collect the two paychecks and let the contracts cancel each other out?

Not according to the legend.

Moran pasted up all the first candidate's posters. Then he retraced his route and tore them all down.

June 28, 2007

Where the Boys Are

A few years back, I was researching a story on the gender gap in New York. Why, in some neighborhoods, do women so heavily outnumber men?

I mined the latest statistics and found one section of the Bronx where the census counted around 146 women and 7 men. It was one of those eureka moments in journalism.

I went up there to see this most glaring disparity for myself—only to discover that, of course, it was too good to be true. The numbers were accurate, all right. But the census tract was occupied almost entirely by a convent.

As any young woman will tell you, though, there is a gender gap in New York.

In the beginning it's different. More boys are born than girls. But sometime before people turn forty, women begin to outnumber men.

In New York, overall, there are about ninety men for every one hundred women. In some poor neighborhoods, the ratio drops to only sixty or seventy men per hundred women.

That's why I was so astounded a few weeks ago when I came across this statistic: For every 100 women living in Lower Manhattan, there are 126 men.

Men now outnumber women there by a ratio usually found only in towns with all-male colleges, military bases, and prisons, and in a few computer geek enclaves in Silicon Valley.

As recently as five years or so earlier, the ratio downtown was an unsurprising 101 men per 100 women.

But since 2000, there's been an influx of well-heeled workaholics on male-dominated Wall Street who want to walk to work. Men twenty-five to forty-four years old have accounted for more than three-fourths of the population increase in Tribeca, Battery Park City, and the financial district.

Carl Weisbrod, who used to run the Alliance for Downtown New York, a business group, told me he was stunned. "I always thought downtown had a high testosterone level," he said, "but this ratio is a surprise even to me."

His successor, Eric Deutsch, said, "It's still a bit of a pioneering neighborhood, and in a pioneering neighborhood you often see more single men and young couples."

Still, Peter Lobo, a demographer who studied the impact of 9/11 on Lower Manhattan, said, "For a normal, non-institutional setting, I would say it is among the highest sex ratios that you would see anywhere."

The real estate market is unabashedly capitalizing on, and perhaps perpetuating, this shift.

A sales pitch for the William Beaver House—at the corner of William and Beaver streets downtown, where the cheapest studio apartment goes for $950,000—features a photograph of two women seductively nibbling corn on the cob and a biography of the building's mythical mascot, a martini-toting beaver-about-town, who reveals that he hangs out "where life is sleek and times are thrilling."

Because numbers can be misleading—remember that convent in the Bronx—I decided to conduct some on-the-ground reporting. Call it research, or bar-hopping. Hey, someone's got to do it.

I interviewed one woman who sells advertising for a magazine and lives in Tribeca with her husband. She said, "I tell my single girlfriends all the time to go out for drinks in my neighborhood because it's where all those rumored-to-exist eligible bachelors are."

Marcus Friedman moved downtown last fall after graduating from Brooklyn Law School. He told me, "Neither me nor my roommates put a large premium on the restaurants and nightlife in the area, as we all work terrible hours. We value how spacious our apartment is, the amenities in our building, and the excellent subway accessibility. Most of the girls I'm cool with," he said, "have a bit more vested in their neighborhood than commute and apartment size. They would rather sacrifice one or the other to have the restaurants and bar scene that they want close by."

Lower Manhattan had changed enormously in just five years, but I wasn't sure what to compare it to.

So I asked a former professor or mine, Andrew Hacker, who's now at Queens College and wrote *Mismatch: The Growing Gulf Between Men and Women.* He described "a jump from 101 to 126 guys per 100 girls in only five years as hyper-unusual." Hacker said a change of that magnitude is typical only in super-booming suburbs in the Southwest.

"Of course," he added, "New York women will tell you that, to them, it looks like two hundred of them for every hundred men. But then," he said, "they mean 'eligible' men."

May 3, 2007

To the Wind

Talk about coming full circle. The earliest painting of Lower Manhattan is punctuated by a windmill—not far from what would become the site of the World Trade Center. Befittingly, New York was only briefly a one-windmill town.

Windmills would symbolize the city's economic supremacy, ensured by the Bolting Act in 1680, which required that all grain exported from the colony be ground in New York. They served as landmarks for arriving vessels and, when the vessels' sails were furled, as an early-warning signal of storms. The centerpiece of the city's official seal, adopted from the Dutch, is still the four blades of a windmill.

Now, nearly 400 years later, Mayor Bloomberg proposes to install wind turbines just offshore—and maybe even on some bridges and skyscrapers—to generate electricity and wean New Yorkers from the nation's polluting and overpriced power grid. He's invited private investors to respond with "expressions of interest" for innovations like wind farms, which could supply 10 percent of the city's power needs within a decade.

Delivered with gusto on the fifth anniversary of a blackout, his bold vision has largely generated a minor tempest among cynics so far and a few bad jokes: Imagine how much more wind power we could produce during a mayoral election year? Or, here's another good idea that small-minded bureaucrats are likely to blow. We've already got Cyclones in Brooklyn. Isn't Chicago the Windy City?

Some critics recall that Manhattan's first windmill, early in the seventeenth century, was a public project that wound up costing the city fathers money instead of generating revenue from millers. A century ago, windmills were briefly considered as a source to power trolley cars, but the idea never gained traction.

The *Times* reported the other day that the search for alternative energy has produced an ill wind upstate, where, in addition to the promise of jobs and tax revenue, the land rush by energy companies has also stirred up a whiff of corruption.

Some earlier attempts at wind power—a lone windmill on a rooftop in the East Village and spinning blades proposed atop the World Trade Center downtown—were abandoned as impractical. For starters, the Northeast isn't as windy as the Great Plains.

And even the American Wind Energy Association, debunking what its experts dismiss as myths about wind power, acknowledges a small potential risk of ice being flung from giant spinning blades and the danger they can pose to bats and birds.

A column on the association's website quotes one estimate a few years ago that wind farms—there weren't that many then—accounted for one one-hundredth of 1 percent of the fatalities to birds colliding with manmade structures. Regardless of windmills, the column said, birds "lead a very tenuous existence."

Want to build your own windmill, but worried about a not-next-to-my-backyard backlash? Here's some advice for the mayor from the Wind Energy Association's columnist: "Get out and meet your neighbors if you haven't already done so," he says. "Invite them over sometime for snacks and beer."

Not too much beer, though. Someone who's drunk—and not with power—is often described as "three sheets to the wind" (an expression variously attributed to poorly rigged sails on a ship, or to a wobbly windmill).

Give Bloomberg credit again for thinking outside the box. We're already tapping tidal energy from the alternating current in the East River to power both a supermarket and a parking garage on Roosevelt Island. The windmill, potent symbol of the city's economic patrimony, might also herald a more energy-efficient future.

When he delivered his wind-power speech, the mayor (who's usually neither blustery nor breezy) hailed the Statue of Liberty as the nation's greatest symbol of freedom—freedom that's being undermined by our dependence on foreign oil. He said he's envisioned the day when Lady Liberty "not only welcomes new immigrants, but lights their way with a torch powered by an ocean wind farm."

In a funny way, we've got the best of both worlds in New York. The federal government is buying about 9 million kilowatt hours of electricity a year from Pepco Energy Services to light the Statue of Liberty and Ellis Island.

It's generated in West Virginia—on a wind farm.

Birds of a Feather

Who knew? New York has something for everyone, but wildlife? C'mon. This is a city that just a generation ago, when the Bronx was burning, defined *indigenous, free-ranging fauna*—in addition to rodents and roaches—as "feral youth."

But in the past few weeks alone, a coyote wandered into Central Park—no one's sure from where—and made himself quite at home.

Herring (no sour cream, just herring) have been (or is it *has* been?) reintroduced into the Bronx River.

Harbor seals were spotted the other day on the rocky outcroppings of two islands in lower New York Bay.

And not only has Pale Male, the celebrity red-tailed hawk, returned this spring like the swallows to his twelfth-floor perch on the façade of an elegant Fifth Avenue apartment building, but he and his mate, Lola, may be expecting.

Naturally, New York was about animals from the beginning. Two beavers adorn the official city seal—reminders of their role in the fur trade. (And we can only assume that the first New Yorkers, when they got frustrated over navigating the city's arteries, exclaimed, "Dam it.")

Oysters were, as a recent *Times* headline put it, the mollusks that made Manhattan, and in the nineteenth century, Mark Kurlansky writes, when people thought of New York, they thought of oysters.

New York is where the cartoonist Thomas Nast sired the Democratic donkey and the Republican elephant, where James Audubon retired to be, he wrote, "soothed by the calm and beauty of nature," where a century ago a wolf belonging to the publisher Ralph Pulitzer terrorized Central Park, where 200 mustangs—horses, not Fords—escaped from a train and stampeded on the West Side, and where, on a winter's day in 1935, according to the *Times*, so this must be true, some kids in East Harlem were shoveling snow into a manhole when they came upon—you guessed it—an alligator in the sewer.

Peregrine falcons have been nesting atop bridges and skyscrapers for a quarter-century. And Pale Male, the hawk, has been a household name for more than a decade. But not even many New Yorkers know that Central Park is one of the nation's top spots for birdwatching.

In 1886, the park's first official bird census counted 121 species. Since then, 282 have been observed. More than 200 species—one-third of all those found in the United States—migrate through this Manhattan oasis. It's to keep them from becoming disoriented that, on cloudy or foggy nights this time of year and in the fall, the tower lights on the Empire State Building are turned off.

Cal Vornberger's vivid photographs of 116 of those native and visiting species practically fly off the pages of his book *Birds of Central Park*. Vornberger, a television and theatrical designer, turned to photography full time in 2001, but he figured the attacks of September 11 pretty much doomed his prospects as a travel photographer. That October, walking in Central Park, he was captivated by a great egret in the Turtle Pond. The rest is history.

In her foreword, Marie Winn says Vornberger's birds are so artistically arranged on their branches or fence posts or hollow logs, doing what birds do best, that "you might imagine each of them flying in for a prearranged sitting at the photographer's studio." She describes him as "a tree in human disguise" who lures birds from their hiding places. "Patience," she writes, "almost beyond human understanding, is his magic flute."

Another new book is Bob Levy's *Club George: The Diary of a Central Park Bird-Watcher*. It's a charming, intimate chronicle of a fifty-year-old laid-off corporate executive's encounter with a red-winged blackbird.

"My behavior changed in significant ways as a direct result of my first interactions with George," Levy writes. "I believe that is all the more remarkable because he initiated those interactions."

His book is as much about people as it is about birds—how human nature helps us cope with the faceless crowd by compartmentalizing it, and how our encounters with wildlife recalibrate our perception of the city.

"I make no claim to have a special skill or talent that attracts birds to me," Levy writes. Instead, he credits Central Park itself: "There are not many places I can think of where so many birds and so many people come into contact with each other routinely."

March 30, 2006

Where America Begins

Welcome to New York. It's what the rest of the country is going to look like not long from now.

The Census Bureau has just fast-forwarded its timetable for America's evolving racial and ethnic upheaval. Experts project that Hispanic people, blacks, Asians, Native Americans, native Hawaiians, and Pacific Islanders will become a majority of the nation's population in 2042. The transformation will occur even sooner for kids—by 2023—and for working-age Americans by 2039.

That demographic shift already took place in New York nearly a generation ago. Sometime in the 1980s, the city passed the proverbial tipping point. The ingredients had been simmering for some time. Decades of white flight, higher birth rates among blacks, and an influx of Hispanic people combined to make New York a majority-minority city.

New Yorkers were a little unsettled by the news. Not just white New Yorkers, either. Nobody wanted the city to devolve into another Newark or Detroit or East St. Louis.

I remember when some civil rights groups even agreed to a quota on new black and Hispanic tenants at Starrett City, the big housing complex in Brooklyn. Their reasoning: If nonwhites became a majority, the neighborhood would lose whatever political clout it still had at City Hall and would go down the tubes.

Today nearly three in ten New Yorkers are black. Almost three in ten are Hispanic. About three in ten identify themselves as white and non-Hispanic. Roughly one in ten is Asian. We've even got more Native Americans than any other city in the country.

New York has not only survived. It's thrived. *On* diversity.

Joel Cohen, professor of populations at Rockefeller University, says race and ethnicity—the whole question of who's a minority—is more about culture than biology anyway. Think back a century ago: Irish Catholics, Italians, and Eastern European Jews, among others, were not universally accepted as white.

I'm identified as white, but when I had my own DNA tested not long ago, the lab found traces of Asian and African heritage. As Professor Cohen says, "All of us are mixtures."

As recently as the 1960s, the census didn't count Hispanic people separately. Asian Indians were considered white.

While defining race and ethnicity as cultural, Cohen invokes a genetic metaphor to explain how diversity has enriched New York and America. It's like "hybrid vigor" in corn—the offspring benefits from the strengths of both parents. Cohen adds a caveat, though: "We need investment in education and health care to ride on the strength of this diversity," he says. "We are neglecting the welfare of our children who are our future population."

Assimilation may have become a dirty word in some quarters, but this city has been reinvigorated by it. Beginning nearly 400 years ago.

While other European settlements were founded by people escaping religious or political persecution or intent on plundering or imposing their own views on the natives, New York was all about making money, about initiative, about getting ahead, and enlisting anyone and everyone who could contribute to that endeavor.

Today, New Yorkers who trace their origin to the Dutch or English are outnumbered by those who describe their ancestry to the census as, simply, American.

As two City University professors and their co-authors point out in their book *Inheriting the City*, "everyone is from somewhere." The latest census projections for the rest of the country just prove what Ken Jackson, the Columbia University historian, likes to say: America begins in New York.

August 14, 2008

A Nose for News

Growing up in Brooklyn, I hated when my mother called me spoiled. The term evoked an irreversible condition, like, say, that of rotting food.

Which brings us to the mysterious smell that wafted across Manhattan recently. It was fleeting, lasting for only about two hours, but it gripped the imagination of New Yorkers much longer.

In this mildest of winters, people have actually begun complaining about the cold, too. Hey, c'mon, it's almost the middle of January ... and the temperature only just dipped below freezing.

And now New Yorkers are also griping that the city smells. Be serious! As an engineer observed on a message board during an earlier nasal engagement, "Gee, a city of more than eight million and somebody just now noticed an odd smell?"

Are we spoiled, or what?

Why our heightened sense of smell?

It's easier nowadays to complain, what with the city's 911 emergency number and the new 311 information line. In fact, 311 gets on average about 50 calls a day about foul odors. That's about 15,000 odor complaints a year, on top of the 28,000 that Con Edison logs about errant gas fumes.

Also, we're understandably more sensitive to sensory stimulation since 9/11. The acrid smell emanating from the rubble of the World Trade Center seemed to linger forever. I remember the quotation of the day three weeks after the attack, by a visitor from North Carolina. "The smell breaks my heart," she said.

Still another explanation for our olfactory infatuation is that while we still fall short of federal air quality standards, the air is a lot cleaner than it has been historically. It's easier to detect a strong odor, whether the aromatic maple syrup smell that pervaded the city briefly in 2005 or the latest wave of gas, which city officials were quick to blame on New Jersey.

People used to routinely dump their garbage on the streets. Thousands of horses and other animals died each year and were often left to rot where they fell. Noxious fumes from slaughterhouses and factories of all sorts emanated from almost every corner of the city.

Today, hardly any heavy industry is left. Most factories that remain are required to install odor-control devices. Vehicle emission standards are stricter, too. Most odor complaints are local, says Geraldine Kelpin, the city's director of air policy, like about garlic from restaurant kitchens.

The Fulton Fish Market recently transplanted itself from Lower Manhattan to the South Bronx. The mammoth Fresh Kills landfill on Staten Island has been closed. A perfume company even began marketing fragrances named for landmark Manhattan neighborhoods.

More than a century ago, the zoologist Gustav Jaeger declared that the nose is the seat of the soul. Every New Yorker has Proustian memories associated with smell.

I always associated the smell of fresh-baked bread with Ebbets Field in Brooklyn, because of a bakery nearby that we passed on the way to baseball games. I also remember the periodic smell from a fat-rendering plant in Queens that the authorities finally closed in 1977.

Dorothy Parker rhapsodized over the "enchanting odor of wet asphalt" on a rainy day. Mention *city* and *smell* in the same breath and other people think of the subway, which is why a snarky New York blog called Gawker introduced a New York subway smell map to pinpoint the most offensive sites.

One great advantage of working for the *Times* is that I could pick up the phone the other day and interview Richard Axel, a Columbia professor who shared the Nobel Prize in 2004 for investigating how people distinguish smells.

"Our nose is not only there to appreciate the emanating odor of a good Bordeaux," he explained. He didn't detect the odor of the other day, but he said "the descriptions imply that whatever it was smelled of gas, or the impurity that we add to gas to give it an odor, and we associate that with danger."

In Professor Axel's mind's nose, New York smells good.

"Much the same way as you associate gas with danger," he said, "I associate the smells of the city with its joy and depth."

January 11, 2007

Early in 2009, city scientists finally identified the source of the mysterious maple syrup smell: seeds of fenugreek, a cloverlike plant used to produce fragrances at the Frutarom factory across the Hudson River, in North Bergen, New Jersey.

Fat City

Here's welcome news for Manhattanites fed up with traffic, congestion, and overdevelopment: Living in Manhattan may be good for your health.

Good, at least, compared with the rest of the city.

The Health Department says New Yorkers have gotten fatter. True, the city is home to a disproportionate number of poor people, who tend to be more overweight. But also of foreign-born, who tend not to be, although the longer they live here the more likely they are to become obese.

Healthy weight formulas vary, but by one measure, if you're 5 foot 9 and weigh more than 168 pounds, you're considered overweight. More than 202 pounds, and you're obese.

Obesity and diabetes are the only major health problems that are growing—and faster here than in the rest of the country.

About one in four New Yorkers is too fat. And in the two years ending in 2004, we—yes, I contributed too—collectively gained 10 million pounds.

Wondering how much more crowded that makes the city? Why you're rubbing up against the next person on the subway or bus? Think of it this way: Ten million more pounds to contend with is the equivalent of adding twenty full-size replicas of the Statue of Liberty. Just imagine she's standing next to you.

We gain more weight for two reasons: We eat more. We exercise less.

"With electric toothbrushes," says Tom Frieden, the city's health commissioner, "we've engineered the last physical activity out of our life."

Overall, more than 300,000 New Yorkers get to work on foot. But Manhattanites tend to walk more than people who live and work in the rest of the city. They're more likely to walk to the bus or subway. Walk up and down stairs to stations. Even walk all the way to work.

They're less obese, regardless of race or income.

While people in certain Manhattan neighborhoods may seem disproportionately anorexic, there's no evidence that Manhattanites eat less than other New Yorkers. And it's the eating—and drinking—that the city's Health Department is particularly concerned about. Drinking soda, especially.

Americans now drink more bottled water than beer. But we consume more soda than bottled water and beer combined. And nearly 70 percent of that soda contains sugar in one form or another. Empty calories, the experts call it.

"Your brain doesn't register when you drink," says Gretchen Van Wye, a Health Department epidemiologist and an author of the latest Health Department fat study. "You're better off eating 400 calories of jelly beans than drinking 400 calories of soda."

The consequences aren't merely personal. Unhealthy people drain the rest of society in medical costs and lost productivity.

In New York, the government has responded aggressively—which suggests why Michael Bloomberg would be less fulfilled as a full-time philanthropist than he has been as a public official.

His generous contributions to worldwide research and education campaigns against cigarettes pale in comparison to the effect he's had on public health as a mayor. He's banned smoking in public places, outlawed artificial trans fats in restaurants, required restaurants to reveal calorie counts, and licensed fruit and vegetable carts in poorer neighborhoods.

Soda is banned in city-regulated day-care centers. But it's still served in schools. And from vending machines. What about levying a sales tax on snacks that are now exempt because they're officially considered food?

"Why should we subsidize unhealthy food by not taxing it?" says Commissioner Frieden, then answers his own question: "I don't see the political will being there," he says.

Sanctimoniously sipping my Diet Coke—but hiding my peanut M&Ms—I told Dr. Frieden that given his puritanical reputation, I'm glad he's not my father.

"My teenager says the same thing," he replied. But, he insisted, he's no Spartan. He likes sandwiches from the Subway chain—he happens to like roast beef more than tuna salad—but because the ingredients are now posted, he also knows that the tuna has more calories. He and his family had ice cream and chocolate for dessert the other night but ate fruits and vegetables, too.

Frieden's prescription? A formula that's usually not associated with New York.

"Everything," he says, "in moderation."

April 3, 2008

Alfred E. Newsman

Guess what Dilip Doctor does for a living. (Hint: His receptionist answers the phone, "Doctor's office.")

"Back home in India, we had a different last name that began with a Z, and in school I would always be called on last," Dr. Doctor, a Queens urologist, recalled. "One day I was complaining to my teacher and he said, because my father and mother were both physicians, 'Why not call yourself Doctor?' That was forty years ago. And then I figured if they called me doctor, I might as well become one."

The Romans called this phenomenon *nomen est omen*. Today's students of onomastics describe it as nominative determinism. Apt names were dubbed aptronyms by the columnist Franklin P. Adams. Once you start collecting them, you can't stop.

Think of baseball's Cecil Fielder or Rollie Fingers, the news executive Bill Headline, the artist Rembrandt Peale, the poet William Wordsworth, the pathologist (not gynecologist) Zoltan Ovary, the novelist Francine Prose, the poker champ Chris Moneymaker, the musicians Paul Horn and Mickey Bass, Judges Wisdom and Lawless, the spokesman Larry Speakes, the dancer Benjamin Millepied, the opera singer Peter Schreier, the British neurologist Lord Brain, the entertainer Tommy Tune, the CBS Television ratings maven David Poltrack.

Think, too, of all those fictional characters and the real-life doctors and dentists named Payne, of Blank the anesthesiologist, Kramp the swim coach, Blechman the gastroenterologist, Faircloth the fashion designer,

Goodness the church spokesman, Slaughter the murderer, and the funeral director named Amigone.

"I once had a doctor named Gore," recalls Anne Bernays, who, with her husband, Justin Kaplan, wrote *The Language of Names.*

Originally, professions were one way of establishing surnames. (There are more than a million Smiths in America, making it still the most common surname, but a considerably smaller number of blacksmiths.) Among collected aptronyms are also nicknames and surnames that were legally changed retroactively and names of people who succeeded in their professions—Dr. Kwak, Judge Lawless, or Orson Swindle, a member of the Federal Trade Commission—despite their names. (Armand Hammer finally bought Arm & Hammer, the baking soda company, after so many people mistakenly thought he owned it anyway.)

What stumps many students of onomastics is the extent to which names become self-fulfilling. After all, Newton Minow did not become an ichthyologist. Paul Bunyan wasn't a podiatrist. Are there a disproportionate number of people named Doctor among medical professionals?

"Some people think I'm a bird specialist, which I'm not," said Dr. Meredith Bird, a Rhode Island veterinarian, who added that she doubted that her name influenced her career choice. "I've loved animals since I was a little kid. But I was forever grateful my mother didn't name me Robin."

"Names and life script, researchers say, are not merely coincidental but, indeed, causative in considerable measure," Professor Ralph Slovenko of Wayne State University Law School has written. "Dr. Robert E. Strange, director of the Northern Virginia Mental Health Institute, tells people that he had no choice but to be a psychiatrist."

David J. Lawyer, who practices in Bellevue, Washington, says, "My routine answer on most days is, I do not know why I became a lawyer. But I do know of people who have been inspired by their names. I was deposing an arborist, a tree doctor, and the guy said his name was Greenforest. I said, 'I get a lot of snickers about my name; you must, too.' He said, 'That's why I chose it.' And I did get a call from a fisherman once with a damaged boat full of fish. It was taking on water, and he goes to a pay phone and all the attorneys in the yellow pages were ripped out, so he looks up lawyer in the white pages and finds me."

Mr. Lawyer said two of his uncles are attorneys, but it's unlikely his three children will follow in his professional footsteps. "They all vow not to become lawyers," he said.

Cleveland Kent Evans, a psychologist at Bellevue University in Nebraska, said, "It is certainly possible that when someone's name corresponds with a word which is associated with a particular interest or profession in their culture, it might make them somewhat more likely to go into that profession. But the people involved themselves would necessarily consciously know that—or consciously want to admit it when it would happen."

Dr. Lewis P. Lipsitt, professor emeritus of psychology at Brown, agrees that the influence of a name is often subliminal.

"You wouldn't expect people to reply that they had a strong awareness of moving toward a profession or occupation or a preoccupation just because their name signified that they should," he said, "but I think there is a real process at work to gravitate people toward occupations and preoccupations suggested by their names.

"I was lecturing to my class one day, telling them to be careful because coincidences do happen. To illustrate, I said I could probably convince you that people's names cause them to go into certain occupations. I mentioned Mrs. Record, who keeps alumni records, Professor Fiddler in the Music Department, Dr. Fish of the Oceanographic Institute. By the time I got that deeply into it, off the top of my head, I'm beginning to think there might be a causal relationship. And then a student said, 'And you, Dr. Lipsitt, you study sucking behavior in babies.' And that had never occurred to me."

February 8, 2007

Angels in America

In 1990, Garcia, Martinez, and Rodriguez were among the top twenty-five most common surnames in America. The government hasn't fully mined the 2000 census yet, but when it does, it's likely that the latest top-ten list will include a Hispanic surname for the first time.

In New York City, for the first time in a generation, the most popular first name for newborn Hispanic baby boys is an ethnic one: Angel.

There are more Angels in America than ever before. Angel ranked thirty-second, a record high, among all baby boys in 2005. (José was still ahead, at thirty.) Angel is now the number one name among all newborn boys in Arizona.

But in New York, the nation's proverbial melting pot, a traditional Spanish name has not been number one, even among Hispanic boys, since the mid-1980s, when José ranked first.

Instead, Hispanic parents generally choose decidedly Anglo names. The latest list, based on birth certificates for 122,000 infants born in 2005, doesn't necessarily suggest a slap at assimilation. In fact, Angel is the only distinctly ethnic name among the ten most popular for Hispanic boys.

Close behind, among the top ten for Hispanic boys, were Anthony, Christopher, Justin, Joshua, David, Daniel, Kevin, Michael, and Jonathan.

Among Hispanic girls, the most popular names were Ashley, Emily, Isabella, Jennifer, and Mia.

What about other New York babies? Among Asians, the most popular names were Emily and Ryan. For blacks, Kayla and Joshua. Among non-Hispanic whites, Sarah and Michael.

Angel is Latin in origin. As a crossover name, it can be pronounced either *Ain*-jel in English or *Ahn*-hel in Spanish. Other than that benefit, cultural anthropologists were generally at a loss to suggest a single reason why Angel ranked first in New York's latest list.

Cleveland Kent Evans, the president of the American Name Society, said Angel is "today's perfect compromise name for those who want to emphasize their Hispanic heritage and yet assimilate into the larger society at the same time."

Hector Cordero-Guzman, chairman of the Department of Black and Hispanic Studies at Baruch College of the City University, said Angel is sort of eponymous and suggestive of "qualities mothers would like their children to have."

I asked Laura Wattenberg, author of *The Baby Name Wizard*, to analyze the top twenty names among Latino boys in New York City. She found that in 2005, 73 percent of the babies received Anglo names, 16 percent Spanish names, and 11 percent crossover names.

"What changed," she says, "was the distribution. Angel rose to the top among Latino New Yorkers by taking a bigger slice of the Spanish-naming pie, not by growing that pie. The rise in Angel is more than offset by the decline in José and Luis," Wattenberg said. "And it's still not as popular as Justin was in 2000."

January 11, 2007

In 2007, an analysis of surnames in the 2000 census found that Smith remained the most common in the United States, but Garcia and Rodriguez had moved into the top ten. In 2008, the most popular names in New York among Asian newborns were Sophia and Ryan; among Hispanic newborns, Ashley and—thanks to Britney Spears and Will Smith—Jayden. By 2016, Olivia and Jayden ranked first for Asians, Isabella and Liam for Hispanic babies.

Black Like Me

Forty years ago, satirizing National Brotherhood Week, the lyricist Tom Lehrer wrote:

> Oh, the white folk hate the black folks,
> And the black folks hate the white folks;
> To hate all but the right folks
> Is an old established rule.
> Today, it's no longer just black and white.

Over forty years, those social distinctions—in New York, at least—have become more complicated. Recently, the legal ones have, too.

A federal judge in Manhattan upheld a defense lawyer's argument that, in effect, not all blacks are alike.

He affirmed a magistrate judge's earlier ruling that prosecutors cannot exclude prospective jurors solely on the basis of their national origin—specifically, that allowing American-born blacks on a Bronx jury, but systematically excluding West Indians, is discriminatory.

Barack Obama's father aside, the growing number of foreign-born blacks in this country may eventually affect white America's view of race. It may also redefine how African Americans identify themselves.

A third of the nation's foreign-born blacks live in metropolitan New York (Miami and Washington rank second and third). More than one in ten American blacks born in Africa and nearly one in four Caribbean-born blacks live in New York—more than in any other state.

In the city, more than one in three black New Yorkers were born abroad—and the share of foreign-born is growing.

More people of West Indian ancestry live in New York than in any city outside of the West Indies. More New Yorkers claim ancestry from the West Indies than from any country except Italy. More New Yorkers come from Ghana than from Canada; more were born in Nigeria than in Ireland.

The recent federal court decision was in the case of a Mark Watson, a Jamaica-born man who is serving up to seventy-five years in prison following his conviction in 2000 for rape, sodomy, and burglary.

Judge William Pauley III didn't find that the Bronx district attorney had specifically discriminated against West Indians. Indeed, a spokesman for the prosecutor says his office never discriminated or condoned discrimination against West Indians or any other group.

But the U.S. Supreme Court has held that blacks, among other minority groups, cannot be systematically excluded from a jury solely because of their race. Peremptory challenges, which require no stated explanation, can be exercised by the prosecution only "to secure a fair and impartial jury."

If prosecutors cannot prove that four Jamaicans and one Trinidadian were excluded from the Watson jury for reasons other than their ethnicity, Watson could be granted a new trial.

As much as the ruling further defines the role that race, ethnicity, and gender can legally play in jury selection, it also speaks to the city's evolving diversity.

Would Watson have fared any differently if the jury had included West Indians?

Michael Taglieri, his Legal Aid Society appeals lawyer, says prosecutors "were deliberately trying to pick a biased jury," but adds: "I wouldn't automatically conclude that my client would lose before a fair jury."

But fair is in the eye of the beholder. And Watson might indeed have fared worse before a jury that included West Indians.

After all, Taglieri cited "overwhelming sociological data that West Indians and African Americans see themselves in economic competition with one another and that a significant number of members of each group have animosity toward the other group."

To put it another way, Donald Keith Robotham, an anthropology professor at the City University of New York Graduate Center, says, "West Indians traditionally tend to have a rather stern Protestant morality, which would have powerfully negative views of rape and especially sodomy, feelings of solidarity notwithstanding."

An enduring issue in New York and elsewhere, as Professor Nancy Foner of Hunter College says, is "that however they identify themselves, how will others view them? Do blacks have the kind of ethnic options that white Americans do? Will they be recognized as West Indian—or African? As black ethnics? Or as black American?

"American society," Foner says, "has a powerful tendency to homogenize blacks, whatever their own preferences."

In other words, maybe Tom Lehrer was right.

March 6, 2008

A state judge decided that the defense failed to prove that the prosecutor's challenges of West Indian jurors were pretexts for discrimination. The case returned to federal court. Watson remains in prison.

Who Counts Most?

You don't have to believe in numerology to know that some numbers count more than others.

Fifth Avenue evokes a very different feel from, as Barbra Streisand sang in "Second Hand Rose," Second Avenue.

The 21 Club—it's at 21 West 52nd Street—has enjoyed a special cachet since Prohibition.

So, to a lesser extent, does the restaurant 212, named for what was once New York City's sole area code.

212, the restaurant, is located in ZIP code 10021, which has always been synonymous with Manhattan's tony Upper East Side. Its residents contributed more to presidential candidates in 2004 than donors in any other ZIP code in the country. Real estate broker Michel Kleier calls it "the most famous and most desired ZIP code in New York City and America."

212, the restaurant, will keep its area code. But it's about to lose its distinctive ZIP code.

About four decades ago, the United States Postal Service codified social class by separating us into ZIP codes. Now postal officials are about to give a new dimension to the adage "There goes the neighborhood." This summer, 10021 will become even more exclusive.

About 50,000 Manhattanites, including Mayor Bloomberg, David Rockefeller, Rupert Murdoch, Ronald Perelman, Spike Lee, and the writers Tom Wolfe and Gay Talese, will be cast from the ranks of 10021 residents—along with Bloomingdale's, Barneys, and the restaurant 212.

They will be ignominiously relegated instead to one of two new garden-variety ZIP codes, 10065 or 10075.

The redefined 10021 will shrink to about 40 percent of its existing boundaries—making it an even cozier Lenox Hill enclave that will boast the Manhattan homes of William F. Buckley and Brooke Astor and also the residents of 740 Park Avenue, who collectively helped elevate that address to what the author Michael Gross proclaimed "the world's richest apartment building."

What with the proliferation of e-mail, it's arguable whether ZIP codes carry the status they once did. What's more, a number of smaller ZIP codes on the East Side, Upper West Side, and way downtown now report higher median household income than 10021.

Still, with the coveted 212 area code (or 917 for cell phones) harder to come by, what's left to hold on to?

Michael Gross told me, "I think ZIP codes matter a great deal, at least as much as area codes and possibly much more," especially to those New Yorkers who now have to adjust to their changed circumstances. "Their *deuxième* ZIP code," Gross says, "will be shoved in their face every day when they look at their mail."

"The truth is," Michele Kleier agrees, "there are some people whose whole identity is their ZIP code."

The Postal Service denies any social agenda. A spokesman insists that growth in population and in new addresses necessitated the change, which promises to be a godsend to stationers. While the die is cast—officially the shift takes place July 1, 2007—former 10021 residents whose engravers cannot meet the deadline will be granted a grace period.

In contrast to the existing 10021, the even more elite version will be denser, with 125,000 people per square mile, and will have a higher median household income, more than $84,000.

How are the soon-to-be outcasts adjusting?

"The first thing you think of is your stationery," Gay Talese told me. "But it's not like an elite number and now you've been demoted. We still have the 212 area code, don't we?" He does.

Tom Wolfe was equally sanguine. "I'll try to take it like a man," he said.

Putting the best face on the situation, Wolfe says he may turn out to be better off living outside the borders of 10021, where the total income is greater than the gross national product of a number of large countries.

"I'm just afraid I can't live up to it," he said.

Mayor Bloomberg, too, seemed unfazed . . . and typically even-handed.

"The mayor doesn't favor one ZIP code over another," his spokesman said dryly.

Howard Rubenstein, the public relations executive, who lives in 10028, just over the existing 10021 border, countenanced calm.

"The same people will be invited to all the fancy parties," he said, "and the fundraisers surely will find their addresses."

March 22, 2007

My ZIP code was changed to 10065. Years later, my monthly bills, addressed to 10021, still manage to find me.

Baseball's Greatest Hit

The call it baseball's greatest hit.

It set a record that would resonate with every replaying but would never be broken. A perfect score.

You won't find it in baseball statistics, though.

The greatest hit wasn't made on the field or even inside a stadium. Legend has it that it originated on a New York City subway.

This week is the one-hundredth anniversary of "Take Me Out to the Ballgame."

On May 2, 1908, the song was registered with the U.S. Copyright Office. On the same day, the *New York Clipper*, a sports and entertainment newspaper, printed an ad for the sheet music, which was published by the composer's company on West 28th Street. It debuted with a public performance at the Amphion, an opera house on Bedford Avenue in Brooklyn. It would be recorded that September. Within a month, it catapulted onto the top-ten charts.

"Take Me Out to the Ballgame" would become, by one estimate, the third most popular song in America, after "Happy Birthday" and "The Star Spangled Banner."

The biography of baseball's anthem has just been retold and elaborated on in a new book, *Baseball's Greatest Hit.*

Thanks to the authors—Andy Strasberg, a sports marketer; Bob Thompson, a New York musician and professor; and Tim Wiles of the Baseball Hall of Fame in Cooperstown—a buried historical footnote has been dusted off just in time to celebrate its centennial.

The song is credited to two adopted New Yorkers. Both transplanted themselves here from Middle America to seek their fortunes. Both changed their surnames to sound more sophisticated. Neither, so the story goes, had ever been to a baseball game.

The lyricist was Jack Norworth, a twenty-nine-year-old actor and monologist, who was performing that spring at Hammerstein's in Midtown, and who had already written another classic, "Shine on, Harvest Moon."

Supposedly, Norworth was riding the old Ninth Avenue El when he spotted an ad for the Polo Grounds, the Giants' home field, in Upper Manhattan. For whatever reason, he drew a doodle of a slightly frazzled iconic New Yorker, whom he named Katie Casey, and wrote in pencil:

On a Saturday her young beau
Called to see if she'd like to go
To see a show but Miss Kate said No,
I'll tell you what you can do—

The immortal chorus followed, including the enviable product placement for Cracker Jack and the "one, two, three strikes yer out," which forever glorified not the hit but the pitch.

The composer was Albert Von Tilzer, a soulful thirty-year-old former shoe salesman in Brooklyn. (As the authors say, there's no business like shoe business.) His music was being featured at the time in a Lincoln Square Theatre burlesque about an Irish politician's son who falls in love with his father's German political rival.

The following year, Von Tilzer would compose another baseball song, after the Chicago Cubs won the World Series . . . for what turned out to be the last time [until 2016]. They managed to capture the pennant by beating the Giants in a replay of an infamous tie game in which nineteen-year-old Fred Merkle was called out after failing to touch second base. Von Tilzer wrote a song titled "Did He Run," but neither the tune nor Merkle's single would become baseball's greatest hit.

Von Tilzer later composed "I'll Be with You in Apple Blossom Time." He also teamed with his brothers in publishing scores of popular tunes that would help enshrine Tin Pan Alley in America's musical history.

May 12, 2007

Scoop

Thirty years ago, while facing down a devastating fiscal crisis, skyrocketing crime, and the growing suspicion that their city had finally proved unmanageable and even obsolete, New Yorkers skeptically tiptoed into a brave new world.

On August 1, 1978, Healthy Law 1310 took effect.

The law would reinstate the tattered social contract. It would profoundly affect individual behavior in public. And it provided an unusually tangible sign that a municipal government seemingly gone mad had finally gotten a grip.

For the first time, New Yorkers were required by law to clean up after their dogs.

Maybe you forgot or weren't living here back then, but the canine litter law raised, well, quite a stink. Of course, letting your dog go just anywhere was never technically legal. Since at least the nineteenth century, New Yorkers were forbidden to deposit "offensive animal matter" on public property. That law, though, was targeted at slaughterhouses and rendering plants and at the thousands of workhorses doomed to die on city streets—rather than at pet owners.

During the Depression, another period in which the reach of government was being sorely tested, city officials embarked on a different approach. New Yorkers were encouraged—required, actually—to curb their dogs, to herd them to the gutter when they had to go. Doomed by traffic, parked cars, and the city's failure to enforce the law and to sweep the streets, the "curb your dog" campaign pretty much failed.

In the early 1970s, under the Lindsay administration, environmental officials Jerome Kretchmer and Herb Elish advanced a bold social experiment: Require pet owners to actually pick up after their dogs.

While New Yorkers like to think of themselves as uniquely creative, the inspiration in this case apparently was a Great Dane in suburban Nutley, New Jersey. Its habit of finding the grass greener on the other side of its owner's fence prompted a local pooper-scooper law.

In New York, the prospect of a similar law unleashed pent-up passions. It conjured up images of an authoritarian regime bent on eventually exterminating every subhuman. Politically, it proved to be even more of a minefield than the sidewalks had become. The City Council passed the buck to Albany.

Paraphrasing that adage about glass houses, Mayor Ed Koch would say, "People who run for office should not throw rocks at dogs."

But with New Yorkers dogged by an estimated 250,000 pounds of feces being deposited daily in public places—that's a total of about 1.4 million tons over 30 years—a canine waste law finally became an idea whose time had come.

Typically, the prevailing popular sentiment was pithily expressed by Mayor Koch: "I don't care if it's good luck to step in it," he said. "I don't want to."

In *New York's Poop Scoop Law: Dogs, the Dirt, and Due Process*, Michael Brandow writes, "New Yorkers were among the first people in the world to bend over and bag the unspeakable."

Since 1978, most of the inventive mechanical devices inspired by the law never proved as popular as a plastic bag or, dare I say it, a newspaper. But despite all the naysayers, the pooper-scooper law has, for the most part, worked—better, perhaps, even than the licensing law. (Health officials estimate that only about one in five of the half-million or so dogs in the city is licensed.)

And since then, the threat of potential punishment, combined with peer pressure, has also had a remarkable effect on public behavior when it comes to smoking, buckling seatbelts, and using condoms. (Though I wouldn't hold out much hope for a similar campaign to discourage jaywalking.)

Still, Brandow writes, no other issue—not even aggressive drivers—provokes pedestrians as much as dog droppings.

"I've been traveling these sidewalks for twenty-five years," he says, "and know of no other aspect of urban life that manages to summon this sort of response. Not the sight of a little old lady being mugged, a child being molested, or a dog being beaten—nothing seems to hold the key to making New Yorkers stop whatever they're doing and 'get involved' like this does.

"I don't like stepping into an unexpected surprise any more than the next guy," Brandow continues. "And I've always picked up after my own. But anything as emotionally charged as this single concern, I've long suspected, just had to be about something more than the obvious."

It was. It was about the boundaries of society's willingness to tolerate deviancy and to legislate civility—one step at a time.

July 24, 2008

What's That Sound?

Call it glamorous. Or, not. But here's what reporters sometimes do for a living.

I stood smack in the middle of Times Square the other day, on top of a steel grating, and asked passersby to identify the sound coming from beneath the street.

Imagine just trying to make yourself heard in Times Square, much less pinpoint a specific sound, whether it's a street preacher or a siren or an impatient cabbie.

You can hear it when you're standing exactly where Broadway and Seventh Avenue intersect, just south of West 46th Street.

It's always there, but what is it? It is sound . . . or noise? How would you describe it?

Here's what some passersby told me: "Are they protesting? I don't know what it is." What does it sound like? "Noise." "I have no idea—I'm from California."

And then every reporter's dream—in this case, an architect from Boston—came along with his family. He remembered the spot from when he worked in Manhattan: that continuous, enveloping, resonating tone that mysteriously creates a sanctuary of sound. And he knew its origin.

Well, two points for the architect from Boston.

Not that all those other answers were wrong. The whole point of Max Neuhaus's sound sculpture is for people drifting or scurrying by to be momentarily diverted and to decide for themselves. In the cacophony of pulsing sound that is Times Square, this *oooom*-like mantra, moan, reverberating bell, modulating tone, organ-like drone—whatever you want it to be—is the one constant. It's literally an island of meditation.

Funny thing, though. Very few New Yorkers or tourists know it's there. It's not on maps. There's no sign to identify it. And that's deliberate.

Neuhaus, a percussionist, composer, and sound artist, told me, "The idea is for people to discover it for themselves. . . . If it were labeled as an artwork by Max Neuhaus, they couldn't do that."

Since it was first installed in 1977, it was discovered by, among others, a subway track worker. He found the phone number that Neuhaus had left on the machine and called him to say, "I don't know what kind of machine this is, but it's making a helluva racket. You better come fix it." It was still working in 1992, but when Neuhaus moved to Europe then and disconnected it, a homeless man moved in.

Four years ago, a gallery owner named Christine Burgin; the Times Square Alliance; Arthur Sulzberger Jr., the publisher of the *Times*; the Metropolitan Transportation Authority; and the Dia Foundation collaborated on a $150,000 reinstallation.

Of course, Times Square today is a very different place from the one that Max Neuhaus helped redefine back in 1977. After 9/11, police wouldn't even allow him into the subway ventilation vault that houses his sound machine—much less tolerate a homeless person living there.

Times Square today is busier. It's brighter. It's safer.

But there is one constant. If you're not on your cell phone or wearing earphones or earbuds, you might pause for just a moment as you cross the crossroads of the world and wonder . . . what's that sound?

March 23, 2006

The aural artist Max Neuhaus died early in 2009, in southern Italy, where he lived. A graduate of the Manhattan School of Music, he was sixty-nine.

Sit Tight

When George M. Cohan wrote "Give My Regards to Broadway," he never figured he would be gone this long.

But his jaunty bronze figure still remains hidden behind a blue plywood construction fence in the heart of Times Square. The statue is accessible only to the pigeons that brazenly roost undisturbed on the songwriter's bare head.

As a *Times* reporter, I have a purview that goes well beyond Times Square. But I do pass through it every day. Things that many New Yorkers ordinarily take for granted tend to pique my curiosity.

A year ago, I wrote about the strange groaning noise emanating from a subway grate on a pedestrian island. It turned out to be a "sound sculpture"—deliberately unidentified by the artist so the source of the sound would be left entirely to the imagination of passersby.

For months, I'd been passing the ugly blue fence surrounding Duffy Square and wondering what, if anything, had been going on behind it.

An ambitious renovation of the temporary TKTS discount theater tickets booth—that old trailer camouflaged by pipe and canvas signage since 1973—was envisioned nearly a decade ago. A design competition was announced in 1999. Nearly 700 submissions, a record at the time, were received. Two Australians won.

"When I started," Nick Leahy, a principal in the Perkins Eastman architectural firm, told me, "I didn't have children. Now they're going to school." Brad Perkins called Duffy Square "the most complex thing we ever worked on."

The project is a joint effort—by the Times Square Alliance, a business improvement district; the Theater Development Fund, which runs the TKTS booth; and the Coalition for Father Francis Patrick Duffy, the World War I chaplain of the Fighting Sixty-ninth Regiment, after whom the square was named.

The coalition originally feared that Father Duffy and his statue were getting short shrift. The development fund was diverted after 9/11. Meanwhile, the price tag increased to $14.5 million, $11.5 million of it from the city.

Ground was finally broken in May 2006. The red-and-white TKTS booth, which looks like the fiberglass hull of a racing yacht, has been installed. Four hundred and fifty–foot-deep geothermal wells have been drilled in the middle of Times Square to provide air conditioning.

But groundbreaking was seventeen months ago. The Empire State Building was finished in less than fourteen months. How did a six-month project that was supposed to be completed last December turn into at least a two-year one?

Well, one of the contractors went bankrupt, and the innovative design has proved challenging to engineer.

Glass panels and beams fabricated in Austria are finally being packed for shipment to New York, to construct what Tim Tompkins, president of the Times Square Alliance, describes as "the Spanish Steps on steroids"—a glowing red glass twenty-seven-step staircase that, as one British engineer boasted, will be able to accommodate 1,500 "fat Americans."

Father Duffy's statue, which was dedicated seventy years ago by Mayor La Guardia and which has been sitting, figuratively, in a Connecticut warehouse, will be restored, with its Celtic cross, to its base.

If everything goes perfectly from now on, the blue fencing finally will be removed next spring.

You can get an advance glimpse, though, in Will Smith's film *I Am Legend*. Smith's character, the lone survivor of a disastrous viral epidemic, walks through a deserted Times Square—deserted except for the mountain lion perched on the roof of the TKTS booth.

A replica of the booth was built for the film in a Bronx armory. It was, Nick Leahy, the architect, says, "the first time I've seen a building destroyed before it was completed."

When it is finally completed 'ere long, Duffy Square may turn out to have been worth waiting for.

For one thing, if George M. Cohan's statue is really as jaunty as it looks, he'll be able to hop off his pedestal and do something that's been virtually impossible to do anywhere in Times Square for years: sit down. Including the steps, the total space available for pedestrians in Duffy Square will have been doubled.

Of course, the whole project is another one of those incongruities of New York. I mean, try asking for directions to Duffy Square.

Like Times Square, which surrounds it, Duffy Square isn't really a square at all. Not in the geometric sense, anyway. It's closer to a trapezoid. And with all the amenities for walkers, the new Duffy Square promises to be anything but pedestrian.

October 4, 2007

Broadway's best seats finally opened in the fall of 2008, after what David Dunlap of the *Times* described as "the longest out-of-town tryout in history." Thousands of New Yorkers and visitors congregate there daily to gawk or just to catch their breath. Like the Metropolitan Museum of Art, the New York Public Library, and the General Post Office, the new Times Square staircase offers a whole new dimension to the New York art form of stoop-sitting. In 2009, vehicles were barred from portions of Times Square, creating even more space to sit and people-watch.

Knowledge of Wealth

I was going overseas some years ago and needed some foreign currency, but the bank branch on Fifth Avenue had run out of *lira*. A teller made the mistake of sending me around the corner, to another one of the bank's offices, in a nondescript building on West 39th Street.

There was no name on the door, just the address. The entrance adjoined a truck bay, which was tightly shuttered. Nothing unusual so far.

But I was completely unprepared for what I found inside. There was no interminable waiting line for tellers, but that wasn't the biggest surprise.

As the polite man behind the counter took my dollars and exchanged them for *lira*, I happened to look over his shoulder. There, piled up on pallets in see-through wire enclosures, were floor-to-ceiling stacks of gold bullion.

One of the keepsakes on my desk at the *Times* is a favorite conspiratorial crank letter. In bold handwritten block characters, the anonymous note confides: "The vault at Fort Knox contains no gold." Still, to most people, *gold* and *Fort Knox* are synonymous.

What's in Fort Knox is chump change, though, compared with the gold bars stored at the Federal Reserve in Lower Manhattan—that fortress-like castle, which bills itself as the world's largest public or private bullion warehouse. That's the hoard that Bruce Willis saves from the evil Jeremy Irons in the film *Die Hard with a Vengeance*.

But the Federal Reserve isn't the only such depository in New York. There are others, just more anonymous.

The biggest one I stumbled on across the street from the New York Public Library.

The proximity of these vast troves of wealth and knowledge conjured up a far different movie in another vein entirely: Francis Ford Coppola's *You're a Big Boy Now*. In that 1960s cult coming-of-age classic, the nineteen-year-old star is a library clerk who roller-skates around the stacks retrieving books.

But just imagine the dramatic possibilities of a remake combining both themes: A geeky librarian tunnels from the stacks under Bryant Park and into the bullion vaults. Like a latter-day Andrew Carnegie, another robber baron, he donates the lion's share of the gold to New York's libraries to keep all the branches open seven days a week in perpetuity.

I went back to the building on West 39th the other day. There's still no name on the door. Five security cameras peer down on passersby.

This time, a guard stopped me in the tiny lobby. What's inside? I asked. "Just offices," he replied.

The bank, HSBC, politely declines any comment on what's behind the nondescript door on West 39th. But the Comex, a division of the New York Mercantile Exchange, acknowledges that the site is its biggest depository in New York. Its website even lists the vault's inventory.

Contracts for precious metals, as they're called, are bought and sold every day, although most of the thirty-five-ounce and one-hundred-ounce bars stay put at the depositories.

At last count, with gold selling at about $760 an ounce, the value of the Comex's 5.2 million–ounce inventory in the Midtown vault is nearly $4 billion. The vault also holds nearly another $1 billion in silver.

"Everything we have is in New York City," says William Purpura, senior vice president of the Mercantile Exchange.

Why keep precious metals in the middle of Manhattan? Purpura says the exchange requires that depositories be sufficiently capitalized and have adequate security and insurance. And he points out that while storing the gold under a mountain in Montana might sound safer, after 9/11 the full $110 million in bullion that was buried under 4 World Trade Center in 2001 was recovered.

In a city that relentlessly tests your mettle and in which political alchemy has been elevated to a science, let's remember the old nineteenth-century immigrant lament: "I came to New York because I heard the streets were paved with gold. When I got here, I learned three things: The streets are not paved with gold. They are not paved at all. I am expected to pave them."

These days, the streets are paved, more or less. Not with gold, but there's more of it beneath them than most New Yorkers would ever imagine.

October 25, 2007

By mid-2018, gold was trading for more than $1,200 an ounce.

North by Northwest

Millennia from now, when archaeologists unearth Manhattan, they'll probably be baffled by the street grid.

Just as we alternately scratch our heads and marvel at Stonehenge or the astronomically advanced Aztec temples and the geometry of the pyramids, they well may wonder what prompted our civilization to rotate the avenues about twenty-nine degrees from the north–south axis.

What arcane mathematical formula governed the grid so that at dusk on May 28 and July 13, and at dawn on December 5 and January 8, the sun would shine from river to river right down the middle of Manhattan's 155 parallel cross-streets?

The rectangular city block was not angled deliberately for the unimpeded arrival and departure of sunlight on those four days. The genesis for the angling is not some biblical injunction or solar cult. Rather, it began with a surveyor recruited from Philadelphia 200 years ago, in 1806. He was charged with mapping most of Manhattan north of Houston Street . . . but he gave up. According to the official version, he informed the city a few months later that he was prevented by sickness from carrying out his contract. Chances are, like other frustrated officials, he fell victim to competing property owners, business interests, and politicians. An early version of "not in my backyard."

In fact, the Common Council complained back then: "[T]he incessant remonstrances of proprietors against plans—however well devised or beneficial—wherein their individual interests do not concur, and the impossibility of completing these plans but by tedious and expensive course of law, are obstacles of a serious and perplexing nature."

So the city fathers did what they often do when they're stymied: They passed the buck to Albany. In 1807, the state legislature authorized a three-man commission to hire its own surveyor. It's probably apocryphal that the commissioners decided on the rectangular street grid after juxtaposing some wire mesh for screening gravel over a map of Manhattan. But that's pretty much what they suggested when, four years later—after their surveyor was frequently arrested by the sheriff for trespassing and had to be bailed out by a former mayor—they issued their farsighted report.

"To some," they wrote, "it may be a matter of surprise that the whole island has not been laid out as a city. To others it may be a subject of merriment that the commissioners have provided space for a greater population than is collected on any spot on this side of China."

The plan provided for a reservoir and observatory, a public market, and a parade ground—but few parks, because the planners figured the waterfront would suffice. They placed most of the streets running river to river because at the time there wasn't much reason to venture north of 14th Street, and because they assumed that maritime commerce would create the most traffic.

The result of imposing a democratic rationality on an unruly city was what one historian called the most radical transformation of New York's geography since the Ice Age.

According to one translation, the name *Manhattan* was derived from Algonquin for "island of hills." Under the commissioners' plan, an army of street openers eventually obliterated hills, salt marshes, cascading streams, and about 40 percent of the buildings that, on the new map, had suddenly become roadblocks.

They were replaced by what one geologist calls a Cartesian flatland, rotated from true north to allow traffic on the avenues to traverse the entire length of Manhattan island, instead of driving directly into the rivers.

The bulky boxes that scrape the sky and the untampered towers that sprout like weeds from lots that seemed to be vacant only yesterday have produced a city very different from the one that once prompted Charles Dickens to exclaim, "Was there ever such a sunny street as this Broadway!"

Now, mostly in the shade and on more level turf, New Yorkers can play taxicab geometry on the street grid, defying the theorem that a straight line is the shortest distance between two points. And four days a year we can engage in that "only in New York" ritual of watching the sun rise or set down the middle of every crosstown street.

June 8, 2006

Christmas in New York

Growing up Jewish in Brooklyn, I was always a little troubled by my disconnect with Santa Claus. How come he never came to our house in Brooklyn? Had I really been that naughty? Had all our neighbors been, too?

Every December, we drove to other neighborhoods—Bay Ridge and Bensonhurst—to marvel at the lavish Christmas displays.

We religiously watched the Thanksgiving Day parade on TV, although even then I was baffled about not only why Santa arrived in November, a month early, but what prompted him to make his seasonal debut in New York.

Let's face it. New York has never been celebrated for either its cleanliness or godliness. You can argue that Santa is more closely connected to merchandizing and gift-giving than to God, anyway.

But what I didn't know growing up in Brooklyn—and learned only recently—is how closely Santa and Christmas have been associated with New York for hundreds of years.

His very name is derived from the Dutch, who colonized New Amsterdam nearly 400 years ago. They christened the character based on St. Nicholas as Sinterklaas.

In 1809, in his lampoonish history of Dutch New York, Washington Irving Americanized and secularized the big-bellied benefactor in the horse-drawn wagon as Santa Claus.

Without Irving, writes the Christmas scholar Charles Jones, "there would be no Santa Claus."

The following year, the *New York Spectator* published what Jones describes as the first Santa Claus poem.

Then, in 1821, William Gilley, a New York bookseller, published another poem about Santa—this one, accompanied by an illustration of a sleigh perched on a rooftop and drawn by a single reindeer.

Clement Clarke Moore, who lived in Chelsea and taught at the General Theological Seminary on Manhattan's West Side, embellished the original image with seven more reindeer and introduced them by name. In his classic poem "A Visit from Saint Nicholas," published in 1823 in an upstate New York newspaper, Moore also provided the proverbial chimney, the oversized elf's infectious jollity, and the requisite bundle of gifts.

About the same time, Moore also wrote what has been described as the first poem written as a letter to Santa—evidence that Joe Nickell, a historical document consultant, concludes helps establish Moore and not another New Yorker, Henry Livingston, as the author of "A Visit."

German immigrants in New York propagated the Christmas tree.

Santa's red suit with white cuffs and collar were popularized later in the nineteenth century by Thomas Nast, a New York cartoonist for *Harper's Weekly* magazine.

The immortal editorial "Yes, Virginia, There Is a Santa Claus" was written 110 years ago by Francis Pharcellus Church in the old *New York Sun* in response to a letter from an eight-year-old girl, Virginia O'Hanlon. She lived on West 95th Street in Manhattan. Her father was a doctor who worked for the New York Police Department. Virginia grew up to become a New York City schoolteacher.

In 1902, L. Frank Baum, the New York native who wrote *The Wizard of Oz*, wrote another children's book, *The Life and Adventures of Santa Claus*.

In 1939, Rudolph, the red-nosed ninth reindeer, was conceived by Robert May, a New York–born advertising copywriter for Montgomery Ward.

And as Michael Miscione, the Manhattan borough historian, says, Irving Berlin may have been channeling Los Angeles when he conceived "White Christmas," but he wrote it in his Beekman Place townhouse, on Manhattan's East Side.

"Christmas may have begun in Bethlehem," Miscione says, "but the traditions that largely define it today came from New York."

December 20, 2007

What Has Four Wheels...?

Not to sound like Andy Rooney, but ... Now that it's getting warmer and buggier, did you ever wonder why relatively few New York buildings have window screens?

The city's Health Department officially recommends that New Yorkers install them, but there are none at the department's own offices downtown (although the health commissioner has them at home in his high-rise apartment). The city replaced a million windows in its Housing Authority apartments but installed window screens in only one of its 344 public housing projects, in the mosquito-prone Rockaways.

This isn't one of those have/have-not stories, though. When the windows at Gracie Mansion—in the middle of a park and near the water—are open, the mayor's official residence is unprotected against houseflies and mosquitoes. The developers renovating the Plaza hotel are negotiating with the Landmarks Commission over which windows to install on apartments that will sell for upward of $33 million. The windows will open, they'll pivot for easy cleaning, but guess what: no screens.

Now, here's another intriguing fact about a government that often seems given to regulate every activity imaginable: Window guards are mandated in apartments where a child younger than eleven lives, and rules defining screens as affixed appurtenances require that they be installed properly. Officials say, though, they're unaware of any rules actually requiring window screens.

The city once proposed requiring screens as an alternative to aerial spraying of mosquitoes to slow the spread of West Nile virus but abandoned the proposed requirement as impractical.

You might say that flying insects played a pivotal role in New York's ascendancy in the late eighteenth century. One reason the nation's capital was moved to New York back then was the mosquito-borne yellow fever epidemic gripping Philadelphia.

By the nineteenth century, screens made from woven horsehair or cheesecloth were popular, but most were used to prepare food or to protect it. Advances in mass-producing wire mesh led to the first patents for metal window screens—including one in 1862 by George Bedford of New York, and another, an adjustable one, patented in 1863, by Lewis Thompson of Brooklyn.

Window screens became popular for a couple of reasons.

For one, factory inventories of wire mesh began growing when the Civil War shut markets in the South. About the same time, brazen Americans became more open to exposing themselves to night air breezes—a cultural reversal that, by the way, had nothing to do with the Draft Riots. And science conclusively established links between flying insects and diseases like malaria and typhoid.

Which brings us back to the question, why not in New York?

Well, one reason is that people don't open their windows. Forget about bugs—they don't want to let noise or smells in or let air conditioning out. For other real and iconic New Yorkers who like to yell out their windows—think Art Carney in *The Honeymooners* or Gertrude Berg's neighbors in *The Goldbergs*—screens would cramp their conversational style.

Some casement windows won't accommodate screens. In some new buildings, the windows don't open. Screens can get dirty and darken rooms. Landlords are afraid screens might fall out and someone will sue.

There's another reason. Frankly, the city probably has fewer flies than it used to. It definitely has fewer horses. In the 1920s, health officials intent on reducing the fly infestation tackled, or at least quantified, one source: They conducted a horse census and counted 50,000 of them. About that same time, City Hall was invaded by mosquitoes, which apparently bred in the pool of water surrounding the statue of *Civic Virtue* in City Hall Park.

We still have puddles of stagnant water. And sewers. And roof gardens. And there's still garbage—remember the joke about what has four wheels and flies?

Theres's still another reason why not many high-rise apartments have window screens, and it's a specious one. Remember that *Cosby Show* episode about the snake? Bill tries to convince his kids that snakes can't climb stairs. Turns out, they can.

Well, flies can fly. So can mosquitoes. And pretty high.

The wind may confuse the bugs about the source of odors and challenge them to reach their targets, but they're light enough to be carried on air currents wafting through the city's man-made canyons. Dr. Jody Gangloff-Kauffman, a Cornell entomologist, doesn't recall screens on any of the apartments where she lived in Manhattan, but she says flies and mosquitoes have been found at least a thousand feet up.

Marilyn Davenport, a senior vice president of the Real Estate Board of New York, recalls being visited by an occasional ladybug—and a starling—in her screenless sixth-floor apartment in Brooklyn Heights.

What about that Health Department recommendation? "All in all," says Joseph Conlon of the American Mosquito Control Association, despite the Health Department's recommendation, "not having window screening is probably not an unduly risky behavior in high-rises."

But Louis Sorkin of the American Museum of Natural History remembers flies in the twelfth-floor apartment he used to rent in Midtown. Now people visit him with bugs to identify all the time.

"If people had screens," Sorkin says, "they'd probably keep out the insects they keep bringing me."

April 13, 2006

An Open-and-Shut Case

How can doormen go on strike?" one New Yorker asked incredulously. "What are they going to do, stand in front of your building?"

That's just one of the many ironies involving doormen. A survey by Peter Bearman, a sociology professor at Columbia, found that while most doormen say they're usually bored, they often seem to be too busy just when you need them. Most say their main job is security, but that often appears to mean protecting tenants from one another.

Residential doormen are not unique to this city, but, as Professor Bearman writes in a new book about them, "like bagels, they are quintessentially New York."

New York has more apartment building employees than cabbies. On average, they make about $37,000 per year, which is more than graduate teaching assistants, bartenders, or travel agents but less—at least before tips—than postal clerks, flight attendants, truck drivers, or fitness instructors.

With landlords concerned about soaring pension and health care costs and demanding a wage freeze, Manhattan, Brooklyn, and Queens residents were contemplating the implications of a walkout: how to survive even temporarily without the 28,000 doormen, elevator operators, handymen, porters, and superintendents who work in 3,500 apartment buildings. After all, we've had residential doormen in the city—well, some New Yorkers have—for about 140 years.

The first reference I could find in the *New York Times* was in 1869. An article about a new concept in living—the apartment house—marveled that "a respectable porter attends to the common door and communicates with each suite of rooms."

It wasn't long, though, before people were complaining about their castles in the air. The upper floors promised less noise and also better air, but, as the *Times* editorialized as long ago as 1883, "the sweller the house and the higher the rent, the more frequently does the elevator cease running and lay up for mysterious repairs." The same editorial uncharitably likened apartment building workers to Cerberus—not the computer program but the mythological three-headed beast that stood watchdog over the Underworld.

There's that occasional nostalgic tribute to the constancy and compassion of the doorman who's retiring, often after decades of largely being taken for granted—one recently decamped from a building near Gramercy Park after forty-nine years. But most seem to achieve their only measure of immortality—as doormen, anyway—when they are quoted about celebrity tenants who disappear or die, or in stories in which tenants gripe about giving Christmas tips to dozens of people they've never heard of or rarely see, or in tales in which pollsters and political candidates—as they have as far back as 1927—grouse about doormen as gatekeepers who insulate potential voters from campaign workers.

During World War II, when some landlords wanted to save money and manpower by dismissing doormen—but without reducing rents—the government went so far as to officially define when a doorman is essential, at least in wartime. Said one federal official, "The doorkeeper who is dressed like a Balkan general and who performs no necessary service, but flatters the tenants' vanity by saying 'Good morning, sir' or 'Good evening, sir' or 'Do you want a cab, sir?' is of course not essential and can be eliminated without affecting the rent."

But, the official added, "the doorkeeper who is really necessary to the smooth running of an apartment house and to the comfort of the tenants; who aids in the distribution of mail, packages, and supplies; who keeps peddlers and suspicious characters out and prevents tramps from sleeping on the red plush furniture in the lobby; who aids visitors in locating the apartments of their friends; who sees that children get safely across the street on the way to school, does perform a real service."

Some wear white gloves. Some sport blazers. At one Park Avenue building, the uniformed doormen still bear a striking resemblance to police officers—a vestige of the 1950s, when the judge who presided over the Rosenberg atom spy case lived there.

When automatic elevators were introduced, they were branded as death traps by tenants concerned about crime. Legislation was introduced to require that buildings with self-service elevators hire doormen.

You may have suspected this, but Professor Bearman concludes that the apartment building lobby is an experiment in sociological synergy. He writes, "Tenants strive for distinction and doormen strive for professionalism. For doormen to be professionals, they must have distinct tenants. For tenants to have distinction, they must have professional doormen."

He also theorizes that doormen are more important than ever in the increasingly privatized, post–9/11 world in which many New Yorkers order in their meals, get merchandise they bought over the Internet delivered, and watch movies at home. Doormen, he writes, "stand between the exterior world of the street and market and the interior world of the apartment and heart . . . or stomach."

A recent story in the *Times* noted that some apartment dwellers prefer buildings without doormen because they don't want to feel obligated to engage in idle chitchat. To which one reader from Brooklyn replied, "What makes these people think that their doormen have any interest in chatting with them anyway?"

Professor Bearman's research reveals another insight: Most doormen wouldn't live in a doorman building even if they could afford to. "Doormen," he writes, "know how much they know about tenants and would prefer not to have someone know that much about them."

April 20, 2006

Eat Your Heart Out

When Marla Maples, Donald Trump's former wife, opened Peaches, a restaurant on Manhattan's East Side, she invoked the fundamentals of *feng shui* to make the place more inviting. Not even *feng shui* could keep Peaches alive. As Eric Asimov wrote in the *New York Times*, the place had the "lifespan of a piece of ripe fruit."

There are 20,000 restaurants in New York, and this is the story of one of them. Actually, it's the story of twelve of them—all at the same location. Depending on how you count, Peaches was number ten. Which is why, as one exasperated former restaurateur put it, "the restaurant business is an oxymoron."

Gay Talese, a former *Times* reporter, has just written an ingenious and engaging book called *A Writer's Life*. It's about another oxymoron—"works in progress"—inspired but unfinished projects that, for one reason or another, never evolved into full-fledged books themselves.

One of Talese's projects was a book about what he calls the Willy Loman Building—a five-story former moving and storage warehouse that was opened on East 63rd Street a century ago by a German immigrant. It was sold in 1952 to an Italian-American trucker whose son and daughter moved to the Midwest, but still own it, and has been home to many failed restaurants.

The first restaurant to open was Robert Pascal's Le Prèmier. The place was so exclusive that it had an unlisted phone number for so-called preferred customers, who plunked down a $500 deposit. It opened in 1977, a nadir in New York City. On opening night, the solid-brass sign over the doorway was stolen.

In her *Times* review, Mimi Sheraton said the décor was dazzling. You can't eat the furnishings, though. She described the coulibiac of salmon as "one of the biggest messes we have ever been served in a restaurant that has the pretensions of this one." She awarded it one star.

Le Prèmier was followed by Gnolo, which was opened by a former headwaiter at Elaine's; Moons, owned by a cousin of *Times* columnist William Safire; John Clancy's East; Lolabelle; Napa Valley Grill; Tucci; and Peaches, which Ms. Maples opened with Bobby Ochs. Talese recalls that Ochs's other claim was that his father, a Bronx dentist, made false teeth that the Russian revolutionary Leon Trotsky was wearing when he was assassinated.

What's made this a loser's location? You can't blame it on the block. The buildings on both sides have about 2,500 apartments. Another restaurant, Bravo Gianni, has been there for more than 23 years. And some other restaurants have survived mixed reviews—the *Times* wrote that the fish at John Clancy's East had not fared well on their upstream migration from the restaurant's progenitor in Greenwich Village and that the service at Lolabelle's was loopy.

Talese's book ends with the impending arrival of the eleventh partnership at the East 63rd Street site, a kosher Italian dairy restaurant named Il Patrizio. The day it opened, the brick pizza oven burned through a water hose and flooded the place.

In 2005, Il Patrizio was succeeded by a kosher Japanese steakhouse, Haikara (Japanese for "high-class") Grill, under the same ownership. It's still open—nearly a year.

The building's lease is held by J. Z. Morris, a real estate tycoon who just moved back to his hometown in Indiana from Florida. Morris recently reduced the restaurant's rent to $15,000 a month.

Haikara Grill's owner is Steve Levy, a former Wall Street broker. You could say he went from common stock to chicken stock.

"I very much believe in karma," he says. "With a kosher restaurant, you have a lot of praying going on, and I honestly believe some of the religious stuff has sunk into these walls."

April 27, 2006

Sunk was the right word. Haikara Grill closed in mid-2007. Steve Levy reopened it early in 2008 as Smokin' Q, a decidedly nonkosher barbecue place. It was the thirteenth restaurant parternship at that site in thirty years. Smokin' Q came with a money-back guarantee: "If you don't like it," Steve Levy said, "give me the money and don't come back." But by early 2009, Levy's Smokin' Q had closed. Levy was undecided on his next restaurant venture but was certain about what he would not do: He would not open another restaurant at 206 East 63rd Street. "No," he told me. "Not even with your money." Maybe the karma will finally click in the site's latest incarnation: It's a Buddhist temple.

New Yorkers

A Place to Die For

It's tough enough to find a place to buy or rent if you want to live in Manhattan temporarily. It's even harder if you're planning to remain permanently.

Sure, people are dying to live here. Not the other way around, though.

The dead have been leaving Manhattan since the mid–nineteenth century. Thousands were transplanted—literally—to the other boroughs and the suburbs.

Health was the ostensible justification, especially after the big cholera epidemic in the 1830s. Imagine, as people were urged to do, how those infected remains might taint the city's already precarious water supply.

But the real reason for banning new cemeteries and emptying the old ones was real estate.

Why bury dead bodies when you could charge lots of real live people, stacked atop each other in apartment houses and office buildings, even more to live and work here?

I was reminded of that history the other day when former Mayor Ed Koch told me he wanted to be buried in Manhattan. After he dies.

Koch is eighty-three. He's lived here most of his life, in a Greenwich Village apartment as a city councilman and congressman, in Gracie Mansion as mayor, and now near Washington Square again, as Citizen Koch.

"The idea of leaving Manhattan permanently irritates me," he explained.

But Manhattan's burial grounds have run out of room.

Only so much space is available in the other boroughs, too.

Brooklyn's Green-Wood Cemetery, home to more than half a million former New Yorkers, says it will stop selling plots in about two years.

Woodlawn, in the Bronx, still has 24 acres left. That should last another two decades, given a density of about 1,000 an acre and the current rate of burying 1,200 a year. Woodlawn also has some space available in private plots. If your name happens to be Farragut, for example, you're in luck. Only four people are entombed in the admiral's family plot. There's room for 32.

Cremation is also extending the life of cemeteries. But Richard Moylan, Green-Wood's president, advises: Watch your ashes.

"Some churches have spots for cremated remains, but they tear down a lot of churches," he warns. "Cemeteries are here forever."

Moylan also is no fan of the ephemeral. "Sprinkle my remains over the eighteenth green? Maybe that seems like a nice idea for me when I'm dead," he says. "But suppose the wife and kids aren't golfers? Death is for people who are still alive."

Which brings me back to Mayor Koch.

Koch said he learned recently from Carl Weisbrod, a former colleague in city government and now the president of Trinity Real Estate, that there's space available in the cemetery that Trinity Church operates at Broadway and 155th Street. It's on the site of a fierce Revolutionary War battle but now offers what Trinity describes as "a special place of peace and tranquility far from the chrome and glass towers of central Manhattan."

The burial grounds of Trinity Church and St. Paul's Chapel downtown include the graves of many historic figures. Among those buried at the uptown cemetery are Clement Clarke Moore, who wrote "A Visit from St. Nicholas"; the artist John James Audubon; the actor Jerry Orbach; and Mayors A. Oakey Hall and Fernando Wood.

Trinity, part of the Episcopal Diocese of New York, is nondenominational and not a Jewish cemetery, so Koch said he consulted with a number of rabbis. "I was going to do it anyway," he said, "but it would be nice if it were doable traditionally."

He was advised to request that the gate nearest his plot be inscribed as "the gate for the Jews." The cemetery agreed.

That may help former constituents, on a pilgrimage, to find him.

"I'm extending an open invitation," Koch said.

Trinity says its uptown cemetery is the only active one in the borough where about one-fourth as many Manhattanites die every year as the number of people who are born.

Still, that's 10,000 deaths a year. And while Trinity's mausoleum offers niches and crypts, only 15 below-ground burial plots are vacant.

Koch said he paid $20,000 for his. A good investment, he explained, given that, unlike the stock market, the price of cemetery space is going up. And, for 234 square feet, it's a bargain. The average price of a Manhattan condo is more than ten times higher.

Anyway, finding the right apartment can take an eternity.

April 24, 2008

By 2009, Koch had installed and inscribed his tombstone and recruited a rabbi to preside over his funeral. He had issued an apology or two, confessed to a few regrets as mayor, and even insisted he no longer carried any grudges—well, maybe just a few. He died in 2013.

The Best Policy

Remember Tom Lehrer's lyrics about the good old American know-how we got from captured scientists?

Once the rockets are up, who cares where they come down.
"That's not my department," says Wernher von Braun.

The speaker of the New York State Assembly has just come up with what sounds suspiciously like a corollary to Lehrer's noncomplicity theorem.

I asked Speaker Sheldon Silver the other day whether New Yorkers should be worried that since 2003, seven assemblymen or senators from the city have been accused of crimes. Those accusations ranged from the spontaneous—punching a traffic enforcement agent or tossing a cup of hot coffee at an assistant—to the premeditated, like Brooklyn district attorney Charles J. Hynes's recent charge that an assemblywoman demanded a custom-built $500,000 house, outside her own district, in exchange for helping a developer get a tract of city land.

Speaker Silver, a Manhattan Democrat, seemed unfazed. He volunteered several caveats: The vast majority of legislators are honest, he said. Some of these even are no longer in the legislature. Some have merely been accused, not convicted. The gravity of the offenses varies widely. And then, echoing Tom Lehrer, he added that the legislature is, after all, a mirror of our democracy.

"We don't pick our members," Silver said. "Members are sent by their communities to the legislature. We just happen to gather together."

They happen to gather together in Albany, where Silver's colleague

David Paterson, a Democratic state senator from Manhattan, had an entirely different reaction:

"I'm amazed at the brazenness of my colleagues," Paterson told me. "There's a higher rate of allegations made against public servants than against the public itself."

He blamed the dysfunctional Albany culture.

"These are people who work very hard and people who are probably underpaid and who many times try to placate the public," he says. "That takes a toll. The passive-aggressive conduct is to feel a certain entitlement."

In the 1970s, Henry Stern, then a member of the New York City Council, estimated that "the rate of indictment of Council members was higher than the rate for teenagers in the South Bronx." (In 2003, after a councilman was shot at City Hall by a political rival, Stern pointed out that an incumbent faced greater odds of getting assassinated than of losing an election.)

Still, in the pantheon of political corruption, Albany has, historically, earned a special place.

Decades ago, state officials detailed a litany of abuse and concluded, "Our investigation establishes that the city of Albany has been had." At which point one investigator interjected, "The question is, was it rape or something else?"

Gerald Benjamin, a political scientist and dean at the State University at New Paltz, says, "People get into politics for a lot of different reasons. One reason is that politics is a path for mobility for people who are less credentialed. People with a high level of energy can get to a position of high status even if they don't have a college degree or didn't go to a prestigious school. It's sort of like sports.

"There is a structural lack of accountability in New York politics, so once you get into office you don't feel threatened, like there's going to be an election or a primary," Professor Benjamin continued. "You become entrenched. The cost–benefit calculus of stepping out of line is affected. Metaphorically, if not empirically, we've come to a point where people are removed more frequently by indictment and conviction than by failure of reelection."

Maybe, though, even with about one in ten members of the city's delegation to Albany accused, legislators are doing the best they can. Speaker Silver says the legislature has already imposed higher ethical standards.

"As far as honesty is concerned, there's nothing we can legislate," he says. "Things are already against the law."

Then again, maybe there's just something about Albany, where, as

Speaker Silver said, legislators happened to gather to conduct the people's business.

In William Kennedy's latest novel about Albany, his hometown, a political fixer named Roscoe Conway muses, "Life without gravy is not life." Later, in a daydream conversation, the pope warns: "Woe to him who builds a town with blood and founds a city on iniquity."

To which Roscoe innocently inquires, "Are you talking about any town I know?"

July 20, 2006

Oh, Albany! Since then charges were lodged not only against additional legislators, but also Alan Hevesi, who was the state comptroller, and Joseph Bruno, who served as Senate majority leader. Governor Eliot Spitzer resigned over a prostitution scandal. In mid-2009, the Senate plunged into a partisan deadlock that redefined dysfunction. And in 2018, former Senate Majority Leader Dean Skelos and Silver himself were retried for political corruption and convicted.

Survivor

L
ots of felons who go to jail find religion to cure their souls. Politicians who are ailing seem to find the mere threat of longer imprisonments to be remarkably therapeutic.

Remember L. Judson Morhouse? Why would you?

But in his heyday, before becoming a historical toenote, Morhouse was the New York Republican state chairman. He was instrumental in electing a novice candidate named Nelson Rockefeller for governor.

Morhouse was later convicted in a bribery scheme to secure a liquor license for the Manhattan Playboy Club. Two days before Christmas 1970, and a month after the conviction was upheld, Rockefeller commuted his sentence. The reason? Morhouse was suffering from Parkinson's disease. Further imprisonment would have shortened his life.

Morhouse managed to live another thirteen years—three years longer than the man who prosecuted him.

Politicians are notoriously windy, but some, despite their convictions, can't seem to finish a sentence.

Morhouse's miraculous recovery was brought to mind just the other day, when Mario Biaggi celebrated his ninetieth birthday in the Bronx.

You may not remember Biaggi, either, but he was a genuine biggie in New York. Hailed as a hero cop—the most decorated police officer. Elected as a congressman from the Bronx, which he represented for two decades. And almost mayor of New York City in 1973, until federal prosecutors leaked to the *Times* the fact that he had once refused to testify before a grand jury.

Personally, Biaggi was one nice guy, immensely loyal and empathetic, beloved by constituents and colleagues. He insisted he was the victim of anti-Italian bias, of guilt by association. As a reporter, I remember imploring him: If you are really innocent, why not prove it by petitioning the court to grant a rare legal remedy and release your grand jury testimony?

Biaggi finally agreed. And he must have been heartned when his case came before a judge who was a fellow Italian. Unfortunately for Biaggi, the judge was Italian by heritage but spoke French at home. He called Biaggi's bluff.

The grand jury transcript confirmed that Biaggi had invoked his constitutional privilege against self-incrimination. He insisted he had fudged only to protect his daughter, for whom he had arranged a job with an ad agency connected to Yonkers Raceway. Prosecutors implied that her salary might have been intended for him, but the grand jury adjourned without filing charges.

In any event, his short-lived mayoral campaign was over.

Biaggi continued to serve in Congress, though, until 1988, after he was convicted in two other cases. One seemed like a cheapo charge: receiving a free vacation from his friend Meade Esposito, the Brooklyn Democratic boss, for arranging government contracts for one of Esposito's clients.

The other was that he had illegally received $1.8 million in stock and cash from Wedtech, a corporation that prosecutors—including Rudy Giuliani—charged had been transformed into a racketeering enterprise that bribed public officials for government contracts.

Biaggi insisted in court that the hostile testimony and unflattering publicity were punishment enough. "I died a little bit every day," he said.

Unmoved, a judge sentenced him to eight years' imprisonment. After a little more than two years, though—six months before he would have been eligible for parole—the judge released Biaggi. He was suffering from what his lawyer described as life-threatening illnesses.

That was in 1991.

By the following year, he had recovered sufficiently to run for Congress again. But his district had been reconstituted, diluting his base. He lost.

Sixteen years later, Biaggi celebrated his ninetieth birthday at a Bronx restaurant with, among other dignitaries, Police Commissioner Ray Kelly and Congressmen Charles Rangel and Peter King.

How did he explain his survival?

"Hey, it wasn't supposed to be a death sentence," he replied. "I returned to New York to get superior medical care."

Which he continues to get. He had surgery recently for colon cancer. He walks with crutches and sometimes uses a wheelchair.

He also still insists on his innocence.

I asked him, if he had been more careful might he have avoided the cloud of smoke that finally led prosecutors to the fire?

"I was famous for being a service congressman," he told me. "What does that mean? That means I went out and got involved in every issue. I would go where angels feared to tread. I functioned on the theory that I'm pure of heart. And how careful can you be? If you're too careful you don't do anything."

Biaggi hopes his epitaph will read: "He cared."

If the turnout and testimonials at his birthday party are any clue, former constituents and colleagues also still care a great deal about him.

Living well may be the best revenge. Surviving isn't so bad, either. After a roller-coaster career, just being alive at the age of ninety may be vindication enough.

November 1, 2007

Biaggi died in 2015. He was ninety-seven.

Being There

New York's last very rich mayor was also self-made. He built his fortune harvesting bat and bird guano in the Pacific. He entered municipal politics, as a snarky *Times* editorial put it in 1880, as a "perfectly respectable man, of no particular ability or knowledge of public affairs" whose only claim to popular support was his expertise at making money.

William R. Grace's wealth itself was not considered a disqualification. Worse, he was viewed as a puppet of the Democratic machine's "Honest John" Kelly. He was a Catholic immigrant in what the *Times* described as an American Protestant city. And he evinced the sort of mind-your-own-business demeanor sometimes associated with wealthy people who aren't used to being held accountable publicly.

He wouldn't reveal where he lived. Or, even whether, having been born abroad, he was a U.S. citizen. "If elected mayor," he replied, "I cannot of course fill the position unless I am eligible and that's all I intend to say upon the subject."

At least Mayor Grace's surname evoked a certain tactfulness. At times, Mayor Michael Bloomberg seemed to have gone out of his way to sound politically incorrect.

Instead of telling constituents bedeviled by adversity that he felt their pain, he sometimes seemed to suggest that they just suck it up. Meanwhile, he graduated from being New York's richest mayor to possibly the city's richest person.

But here's a twist. In response to a benchmark opinion poll measure of empathy, a growing share of his constituents—regardless of their own income—say he cares about the problems and needs of people like them.

Early in his first term, only about one in twenty New Yorkers making less than $30,000 said he cared. Comparing *Times* polls, I found that now about one in four does—nearly the same proportion as among people who make more than $75,000. To put it another way, five years ago 44 percent in the lower income group said the mayor cared "not at all" about their needs. Now, only 12 percent say so.

Don't forget that early on, when other New Yorkers were girding for a transit strike, Bloomberg bought a $600 24-speed mountain bike. Two summers ago, he did the politically unpardonable—he congratulated Con Edison for containing a blackout in Queens. When parents complained about sweltering classrooms, he replied: "People of my generation went to schools without air conditioners. . . . I think it's fair to say that if we closed the schools, most of the kids would be out there playing in the sun."

Responding to complaints that playground equipment gets dangerously hot in the summer, the mayor said recently: "If it's hot, don't sit on it. Air conditioning the slide is not something we can afford to do."

So why the about-face in the polls?

Thing have gotten better for many New Yorkers. Accustomed to political pandering, they've become more receptive to Bloomberg's unvarnished common sense. Maybe the mayor succeeded in lowering expectations about what government can deliver. Risking political capital on public education and poverty, he also deftly cultivated his persona as a subway-riding "Mayor Mike."

Bloomberg now has historically high approval ratings, says Doug Muzzio, a Baruch College political scientist, but "people can't tell you why they approve and on specific matters they disagree. It's almost as if they've bought into the notion of the technocratic philosopher-king, that being wealthy, being a plutocrat somehow allows him to determine the public good."

In 2003, when the mayor was boldly raising property taxes to close huge budget deficits he had inherited—and before he supported tax rebates—Alan Brinkley, the Columbia historian, commented: "He almost seems not to care very much about what people think of him, which in a way is admirable."

"I would not say that about Bloomberg now, although I still think he does not behave like a typical ingratiating politician," Professor Brinkley told me the other day. "In many ways, that may be a reason for his great success."

August 7, 2008

No More Bull

You could argue, as Herman Badillo did to me the other day, that Norman Mailer cost him the mayoralty of New York City in 1969.

You could make a case, too, that Mailer's candidacy assured the re-election of Mayor John V. Lindsay. From Lindsay, you could even draw a wobbly line to the city's fiscal crisis in the 1970s, to its fall and rise, to a conservative backlash that elected Rudy Giuliani, and to a period of postracial politics.

That's all conjecture, though.

What's indisputable is that long before Stephen Colbert flirted with entering the 2008 presidential campaign, voters had never seen anything quite like the 1969 New York mayoral race.

Mailer, who died last week, was perhaps the greatest writer since Winston Churchill to seek elective office. If that weren't disqualification enough, he had also been convicted of stabbing one of his wives. He promised that, if elected, he would at least deliver the bad news couched in "elegant language." But he also delivered sufficient vituperative offense to fill a devil's dictionary of political incorrectness.

Even his three-word campaign slogan—a vulgarization of "No More Bull"—was unprintable. "The difference between me and the other candidates," Mailer once said, "is that I'm no good and I can prove it."

His running mate for City Council president was the columnist Jimmy Breslin, who suspected the worst from the very beginning: that Mailer was serious.

Mailer's own inner circle was deadlocked on flipping the two candidates—running Breslin for mayor and Mailer for Council president. But as Joe Flaherty, the campaign manager, patiently explained, "You just can't shuffle National Book Award winners around like subservient aldermen."

By the way, however the candidates fared politically, the campaign didn't hurt their two bestselling books at the time, Mailer's *Armies of the Night* and Breslin's *The Gang That Couldn't Shoot Straight*—a prequel of sorts to his latest likely bestseller, *The Good Rat*. It's also about organized crime, not about the '69 campaign.

The 1969 race had its share of personalities, if you can call them that. But as Flaherty would later write, it was "a dull campaign in a sad city with a grimace of despair carved into its face. Mailer and Breslin managed, for a short season, to turn that grimace into a grin."

Breslin recalls Mailer's arguing brilliantly at Brooklyn College that the minds of white and black kids would grow best if they were together in the same classrooms. One student interrupted: "We had a lot of snow in Queens last year and it didn't get removed," he said. "What would you do about it?" To which Mailer, abruptly dislodged from his lofty oratorical perch, replied in kind. He would melt the snow, he said, by urinating on it.

Mailer's political nadir was a campaign rally at the Village Gate, where he vilified his own supporters as "spoiled pigs." Breslin left the rally early. He later told a friend, "I found out I was running with Ezra Pound." Breslin was referring not to Pound's poetry but to his insanity.

The campaign was not without substance, though.

Mailer's "left-conservative" platform called for a monorail, a ban on private cars in Manhattan, and a monthly "Sweet Sunday," on which vehicles would be barred from city streets, rails, or airspace altogether.

He championed self-determination—the city itself would secede and become the fifty-first state—an idea rooted, in part, in New York's pre–Civil War greed for the profits from southern cotton. Individual neighborhoods would be empowered to govern according to their own prerogatives, which could range from imposing compulsory free love to mandatory church attendance.

Mailer so gushed with ideas that when the campaign could finally afford an ad in the *Times*, he crammed it with so much tiny text that, as Flaherty recalled, "it probably was the first political ad in the *Times's* history it didn't have to microfilm."

The Democratic frontrunners for mayor that year were Herman Badillo, then the Bronx borough president; Mario Procaccino, the comptroller; and former mayor Robert F. Wagner, whose reelection campaign against the Democratic machine eight years earlier helped pave the way for the 1969 free-for-all—a primary field finally winnowed down to five candidates, including himself. He had been urged to return from Spain, where he was the U.S. ambassador, to save the city from Lindsay.

Wagner was a measured, largely underrated political figure whose credo was "When in danger, ponder; when in trouble, delegate; when in doubt, mumble."

Procaccino might have fared better if he had mumbled. He was prone to malapropisms, once boasting of his racial sensitivity, repeatedly declaring that "my heart is as black as any man's."

Mailer was impressed with Badillo but belittled Wagner as an anachronism and considered Procaccino a buffoon. "I can't get a grasp on a mind this small," he said.

But Procaccino rode a law-and-order backlash to win the nomination, although he would lose the following November to Lindsay.

"Procaccino was not a performer who would win cheers in an open, lighted tent where one's applause signifies allegiance," Joe Flaherty wrote. "But the voting booth is not a bright big top. It is a dark confessional with a curtain to muffle the blackest intents of the soul."

Mailer ran fourth, with 41,000 votes, or about 5 percent, just ahead of James Scheuer, a wealthy Bronx congressman who had spent considerably more.

Breslin came in fifth in a field of six, with more than 75,000 votes, or 11 percent. He would later say he regretted having beaten the only black candidate in the race, Charles B. Rangel. But he was immediately remorseful for another reason entirely. "I am mortified," he said, "to have taken part in a process that required bars to be closed."

Why did he run? "I think the question is," Breslin told me, "why so many others haven't got the personality or guts to even think of trying."

What did they accomplish? "We got a tremendous amount of self-confidence in dealing with politicians from then on," he said.

Given their subsequent successes as writers, wasn't it lucky they both lost?

"It wasn't luck," Breslin replied.

November 15, 2007

Pay as You Go

New Yorkers are consumed these days by their elected officials' expense accounts.

We've learned that while former Governor Eliot Spitzer spent a fortune hiring high-priced prostitutes, he frugally dispatched one woman from New York to an assignation at the Mayflower Hotel in Washington on the cheaper regional train instead of splurging on the Acela.

Governor David Paterson just got around to reimbursing his campaign's American Express Platinum Card account for two stays, five years or more ago, at a Days Inn on the Upper West Side—a hotel where he carried on an extramarital affair and was billed $253 for *two* nights (compared with the Mayflower, where the cheapest double *starts* at more than $400).

Full details of these transactions and others may yet yield a trove of additional insights into the character of the two governors. But, meanwhile, another public official has all but gotten a free pass over one aspect of his personal finances.

Nobody outside Michael Bloomberg's tight inner circle knows how much he spent not running for president.

We don't know how much his noncampaign cost.

We don't know who got paid—or for doing what.

Nor, under the law, are we entitled to.

Campaign financing experts say Bloomberg is under no legal obligation to disclose his expenses because, as a self-made billionaire, he never solicited contributions from anybody else. He never formally declared that he was even exploring, much less embarking on, a presidential campaign.

Nobody is claiming that Bloomberg spent his money improperly.

But if a byword of accountability is to follow the money, where does nondisclosure leave us in a year when we've parsed the campaign financing filings of the other candidates even to compare what they've spent on doughnuts?

If you are what you eat, or what you wear, aren't you also what you spend?

With Bloomberg, we're talking about a guy who invested $160 million on his two mayoral campaigns, which is more than either Hillary Rodham Clinton or Barack Obama reported spending by late March 2008 on running for president.

We're talking about a guy who recently gave $500,000 to Albany Republicans—ostensibly to help them retain their tenuous grip on the state Senate, but perhaps also as an unspoken incentive to approve the mayor's congestion-pricing charge for motorists entering Manhattan.

What's $500,000 to Bloomberg?

That's how much extra he spent in a single afternoon—on Election Day 2001—when last-minute polling suggested he needed to galvanize every one of his potential supporters.

To Bloomberg, spending $500,000 is comparable to a measly millionaire's shelling out a mere $100. That much would buy you a dozen drives into Manhattan once congestion pricing is imposed, but not even a full night at a Days Inn.

The mayor has sort of revealed the recipients of his generous and influential philanthropy. But when I asked Stu Loeser, his spokesman, for an accounting of Bloomberg's national political expenses, he replied, "No thanks. We decline to comment."

Campaigning is expensive.

It was humanizing to hear that in 2001, when Bloomberg was still trailing his chief mayoral rival by double digits, he confided to his pollster, "I'm already in this race for $20 million; when do I start to move?"

Four years later, Bloomberg barely winced when his reelection campaign invested more than $10 million on developing a computerized database that included sophisticated psychological portraits of New York City voters.

After that election, a spokesman responded to criticism of Bloomberg's record campaign budget by suggesting that the mayor had gone beyond the legal requirements in revealing what he had spent.

"The Bloomberg campaign is disclosing the same financial information, in the same publicly accessible format, as all other campaigns," the spokesman said, "even though we are not accepting taxpayer money."

In 2005, though, unlike in 2001, Bloomberg was required to make such disclosures to the city's Campaign Finance Board.

If, as his spokesman seemed to suggest, he was voluntarily doing the public a favor back then, why not now?

March 27, 2008

Instead of running for president, Bloomberg successfully lobbied to extend term limits so he could seek reelection in November 2009. He spent more than $100 million on his successful campaign for a third four-year term.

Crimes of the Century

Think a roguish Johnny Depp or Burn Gorman, who played Mr. Guppy in Masterpiece Theater's version of *Bleak House*. Then you'll be better able to imagine George Appo.

And conjuring up George Appo, as Timothy Gilfoyle does in his new book, *A Pickpocket's Tale*, pries open a grimy, probably broken, window on nineteenth-century New York's netherworld of crime and on the motley denizens of both sides of the penal system.

It's not a pretty picture. But it's a prism that puts today's street crime and white-collar corruption in sharp relief.

George's father supposedly named him for the nation's first president. (Ironically, the city's police chief was George Washington Walling.) But any similarity—especially any involving the I-cannot-tell-a-lie mythology—ended at birth.

By the time George was three years old, he was already behind bars—for his own protection, after his father was arrested for murdering their landlady on the Lower East Side. That was the last time George had to be protected from the public. All of his subsequent stays as a guest of the state were to protect the public from him.

His father earned the distinction of being the first Asian convicted of a capital crime in New York. George was a trailblazer, too. He perfected the art of pickpocketing. As an habitué of opium dens, he was the model for the drug-addicted criminal. He lost an eye—a serious handicap for a pickpocket—and graduated from street crime to less punishing confidence games. He was a self-described "goodfellow" and "nervy crook" who avoided violence and survived by pluck and wit. Like his father, he was judged criminally insane. He ratted on his partners in crime. Then he wrote about them. And, finally, he became an advocate for ex-cons.

He was also a minor celebrity—a reminder that even a century ago, crime was often glorified. A select rogue's gallery of unabashed criminals, among them the infamous fence Marm Mandelbaum, captured the public's imagination. In some cases, they captured something extra: a place in more or less polite society.

Gilfoyle's book provides several other insights into late-nineteenth-century New York: the systemic police corruption; the rampant street crime committed by teenagers; the attempts at rehabilitation; the prisons for which the term *correctional institutions* seems even more a misnomer than it does today; and, in a world without credit cards, the vast amounts of cash that people carried around.

"George's life embodied the changing structure of crime and punishment in 19th-century America," Gilfoyle writes, including "the persistent failure of municipal law enforcement to deter criminal behavior," the "birth of Gotham's first 'bohemia' and a new recreational drug culture," and the "emergence of the professional criminal connected to a national network of illegal activity.

"George Appo—marginalized, ostracized and criminalized in his time, forgotten in ours," the author concludes, "speaks to us a century later in unexpected ways."

Gilfoyle teaches history at Loyola University. He wrote about prostitution in an earlier book, *City of Eros*. In *A Pickpocket's Tale*, which I reviewed in the *Times*'s City section, he injects the requisite academic analysis and lots of footnotes. But some of the most compelling words are George Appo's own, from his unpublished memoirs, which Gilfoyle found at Columbia University. Excerpts whet the appetite for—listen up, Johnny Depp and Burn Gorman—the annotated *Autobiography of George Appo*, which Gilfoyle edited and plans to publish.

George Appo's life, Gilfoyle writes, was a mixture of the apocalyptic and the absurd: He never attended a day of school but wrote an autobiography; he met his father in prison and again in an insane asylum; he was a subject of experimental reforms in juvenile justice but later served two terms at Sing Sing.

In 1930, George Appo died in Manhattan's Hell's Kitchen. After surviving suicide attempts, imprisonment, commitment to an asylum, and more than a dozen assaults, including bullet wounds to his stomach and head, he finally succumbed to what, at the time at least, was considered old age. He was seventy-four.

July 27, 2006

Articles of Faith

Long before there was The Donald, there was THE McManus.

A century ago, New York's political elite was celebrating Thomas J. McManus's epochal defeat of the legendary George Washington Plunkitt for Democratic district leadership in Hell's Kitchen, on Manhattan's West Side.

Plunkitt of Tammany Hall was famous for his political candor, typically delivered at the shoeshine stand of the New York County Courthouse—his defense of what he called honest graft and his famous credo "I seen my opportunities and I took 'em."

Plunkitt also complained, "Caesar had his Brutus; I've got my 'THE' McManus."

Think politics is tough today? On the day McManus won, a hundred years ago, police were swamped with two riot calls, fifty arrests, and the candidate's announcement that he had been targeted for assassination. I guess that's why they called it Hell's Kitchen.

The McManus, as he was universally known, would rule the district until his death in 1926. He was succeeded first by his brother, then by a cousin, then by his nephew Gene.

Heeding Gene's deathbed warning, his son Jim campaigned to succeed him on the day of Gene's funeral in 1963. "I buried my father," he recalled, "and on the way back I was dropped off to see two county committeemen." Jim won. He's presided over the district ever since.

Why have the McMani—as Daniel Patrick Moynihan, a son of Hell's Kitchen, used to call them—survived for more than a century?

Politics, Jimmy McManus says, is his life. He learned to embrace all potential supporters—the waves of new immigrants and the gangsters who gravitated from the waterfront. When I interviewed him for a profile in the *Times*, he told me:

"We didn't interfere with the mob on the docks and they didn't interfere with our politics. Once, they brought an old man into the club who needed a place to live. I said, 'What was your profession?' He said, 'Pickpocket, but I can't work anymore because my eyes are going. But I never robbed a working guy in my life.' I got the guy an apartment."

At seventy-one, McManus is the family patriarch. His niece is his co-district leader. He collects a pension from his patronage job at the Board of Elections. (He told me, "I went in every day, but I could always leave if I had to.") And he also still runs the family funeral home. As gentrification shrinks his traditional political base and makes it harder to bury his enemies for fun, owning a funeral home still places him in the enviable position of burying his friends for profit.

Once, when McManus was running for reelection, nine relatives and friends who signed his nominating petitions listed the building that houses the funeral home as their address. His lawyer explained, "In the old days, we used to vote the graveyards. Jim is a reformer. He votes the funeral parlor."

He told me, "I wouldn't do anything for money that I wouldn't do for nothing."

I asked him what he meant.

"What I mean is, a little old lady comes in and wants a favor. I do it. A big law firm wants a favor. I say, buy fifty tickets for my cocktail party. They're not bribing me. They're just supporting me," McManus said.

But Jim McManus says power has shifted from party leaders to ungrateful elected officials—officials who quickly forget the people and the politicians who helped elect them.

The recent centennial of The McManus's election was bittersweet: The Times Square neighborhood has gotten so good that rents are up and the McManus Democratic Association was kicked out of its storefront. The clubhouse moved into an office building down the block.

Still, constituents keep coming. Jim McManus showed off the cluttered back room—"You can't do politics without a back room," he says—and the telephone also rings in Mr. McManus's apartment six blocks away, just as it did a century ago in The McManus's flat.

"The McManunses," he says, "are always there for you."

March 9, 2006

In 2017, Jim's nephew and niece Mickey Spillane Jr. and Denise Spillane lost the district leadership, leaving Hell's Kitchen without a McManus at the party's helm for the first time in eighty-two years.

American Gangster

Helen of Troy was famous as the face that launched a thousand ships.

You might call Nicky Barnes the face that launched a thousand flips.

Barnes ran what federal prosecutors called "the largest, most profitable and most venal drug ring in New York City." But they couldn't convict him.

In 1977 he begrudgingly posed for the cover of the *New York Times Magazine*. His smug photograph appeared next to the headline "Mr. Untouchable."

President Jimmy Carter was so outraged by the notion that Barnes was beyond the reach of justice that he ordered the U.S. Attorney's Office to prosecute Barnes to, as they say, the fullest extent of the law. They did. He was convicted and sentenced to life without parole.

While Barnes was languishing in prison, he felt betrayed by his former confederates. He flipped—turned into a federal informer. His testimony convicted scores of drug dealers.

In 1998, Nicky Barnes was released into the Federal Witness Protection Program. He disappeared, living with a new identity in what he told me recently is "the anonymity that cloaks middle America."

Now he's making a comeback of sorts, in a new autobiography, *Mr. Untouchable*, written with Tom Folsom, and in a documentary film of the same name. Cuba Gooding Jr. plays Barnes in the feature film *American Gangster*, which, to Barnes's exasperation, revolves around his chief rival in Harlem, Frank Lucas.

I flew to somewhere in middle America to interview Nicky Barnes, to ask him whether he is a changed man or a man who has pragmatically adjusted to his changing fortune. Are the book and film all about ego?

"Ego?" he replied incredulously. "That's not what I need, not with gas at three dollars. I need bank, and this is my only way to get it."

The seventy-four-year-old man who used to be Nicky Barnes once owned sixty pairs of custom-made shoes, twenty-seven full-length leather coats, and more than one Mercedes-Benz. Now he wears baggy Lee dungarees and drives to work in a used car he bought five years ago.

He watches basketball on television. He loved *Little Miss Sunshine*. He writes rap lyrics.

But just raise the right—or, rather, the wrong—subject and he turns into the spitting image of Nicky Barnes. He launches into a tirade laced with aphorisms from Machiavelli and liberally punctuated with an expletive that evokes Oedipal incest.

I asked him, for instance, whether he had ever been framed by the authorities. He referred me to the prosecution that resulted in the life sentence. He said that federal agents eavesdropping on his cronies mistakenly transcribed the word *payroll* as *kilo*:

"This case right here! This case right here! The Constitution doesn't allow prosecutors to convict people because they're doing something morally wrong. Yeah, I was a drug dealer, and I was doing everything they said I was doing. But they didn't catch me at it. I'm not saying I was innocent. I'm saying with all I was doing, they could not get a conviction without a contrivance."

I asked him whether there is anything worse than being an informer.

"Being in prison for the rest of your life. I'd rather be out as a witness than be in there and what they characterize as a stand-up guy."

Or, as he said of his former colleagues, "I'm out. They're in."

Back in 1977, before he went "in," he posed for two *Times* photographers. Once on the steps of the courthouse. The photographer was chasing him and dropped one of his cameras. Barnes said he felt so bad for the guy that he offered to pay for a new one. The photographer had a counter-offer: Let me take your picture. Barnes agreed.

But what about the *New York Times Magazine* cover, the photograph with the "Mr. Untouchable" headline that infuriated Jimmy Carter?

David Breitbart, who was Barnes's lawyer, remembers when a *Times* editor called and asked Barnes to pose for the photo. With his client awaiting trial, Breitbart turned thumbs down. But then, he said, the editor told him that if Barnes didn't pose, the magazine would run his mug shot on the cover instead.

To which Breitbart replied, "What time will the photographer be here?"

This time, Barnes agreed only to be interviewed. But not photographed.

March 8, 2007

A Satisfying Life

David Halberstam was haunted by the odds that he would die young, as his father did. But he survived covering civil rights violence in the South, and wars in the Congo and Vietnam. Only after suffering a heart attack did he seriously begin to confront the challenge of growing old.

On April 23, 2007, just after his seventy-third birthday, the journalist, historian, wise man, and my friend was killed in a car crash in California.

No advance obituary had been prepared by the *Times*. As one editor explained, David Halberstam, by his own example, was not an old man.

He died on the job, having just completed the last installment of his trilogy on lost causes—*The Best and the Brightest, War in a Time of Peace*, and, now, *The Coldest Winter*—and as he was being driven to an interview for what would have been his twenty-second book.

He was born in the Bronx, raised in Westchester and Connecticut, where Ralph Nader was a schoolmate, and became managing editor of the student paper at Harvard, where, he once confessed, he graduated in the bottom third of his class. He deliberately apprenticed himself in the Deep South, where he knew no one, and where his Harvard degree might be considered a handicap.

"I suspect that you in the audience may look at us upon the stage and see people who seem like we have always succeeded," he said years later as a commencement speaker at Skidmore. "Would that that were true. What you do not see is our own anxieties. You do not see me, at the moment a few days short of my twenty-second birthday, when the editor of the smallest daily in Mississippi came and told me that it was time for me to leave. Fired, as it were—for stubbornly refusing to compromise my integrity—from the smallest daily in Mississippi after less than a year as a journalist. What an auspicious way to start a career!"

By the time he was recruited to the *Times*, he recalled, "I not only was a good reporter. I had utter confidence in my ability." To put it another way, he said, "I am immune to bullying."

By anyone. He was irreverent *and* patriotic. And when President Kennedy personally demanded that David be fired because of the doubts he was reporting about America's misadventure in Vietnam, Punch Sulzberger, the *Times*'s publisher, refused.

Unusually generous and a gentleman, David could also be brutal in holding others to account and in viewing ballplayers, statesmen, even offending passersby in vivid black or white. But he also demanded perfection of himself—whether grilling a source or a steak.

He had been hired as the *Times* was evolving from what was arguably a stenographic paper of record into one that valued literary as well as reportorial skills. Or, as he put it, "the old sins were about getting something wrong. The new sin is to be boring."

He said he never thought of himself as a stylist, that "I always thought my job was to work hard, do the interview, get the anecdotes and insights, and if I did that, I could work up a pretty good story."

But he did have style.

He wrote of one man who "always came equipped with his own precipice from which to jump," and another who was "the kind of person who could go in a revolving door behind you and come out ahead of you."

He also had class.

Imposing and armed with a stentorian voice so deep, as Clyde Haberman wrote in the *Times*, that it seemed to start in his ankles—he always marveled that while he might be mistaken for a scion of the American establishment, he was the grandson of immigrants.

He was fascinated by ordinary people's rising to the occasion.

A few years ago I asked him about that. He had earlier said he was always impressed by uncommon men and women and their deeds, whether in Vietnam or in government or in sports or on 9/11 in a firehouse on Manhattan's West Side. Are they uncommon or are they common?

Halberstam replied: "They're uncommon because their life is about risking their lives in a time of peace, which almost nobody else does, and it's about built-in sacrifice and the possibility of death, and it's the nobility of ordinary people which again and again moves me. I've done this, I've been a reporter for forty-seven years, and there are moments where you just see people rise above who they are.

"I mean, there's a crisis and someone who isn't supposed to be a great heroic figure does the right thing and stands up to pressure in a small town in Mississippi or some of the young people I covered who were the first sit-in kids in Nashville and they were Freedom Riders, I mean going into Alabama and Mississippi and risking their lives, they were very ordinary people. They were children of the poorest people in America, black families, parents, had mostly fifth-grade educations, their parents' economics were off the books. I saw this again in Vietnam and not just people doing battlefield valor, but those officers in the field, when their superiors were lying about whether the war was being won or not, refused to be bent even though it might damage their careers and cost them getting a star, and they would say, 'No, we're losing the war,' and they became sources of mine, so it's that kind of nobility that I find thrilling and I found it in the firehouse."

He was impassioned, skeptical, but not cynical. Above all, profoundly curious.

Of Halberstam's insightful book about the Balkans, Richard Bernstein wrote in the *Times*, "He uses mostly interviews with the actors of the time to reconstruct not just the actions they engaged in but also their states of mind, the fears that haunted them, the ambitions that drove them, and the private histories that influenced their public performances."

And his own fears and ambitions?

Lots of kids dream of playing center field for the Yankees, he once said, but how many get to do it, and even then, for how long? He played on his own field of dreams for fifty years, without ever growing old.

"Doing something that you like," he said, "something that you value, something that—even though it is not as sexy as being a television reporter or makes as much money—remains with a resonance within the society, allows you to feel good about yourself, have pride in your craftsmanship that you're serious and that you can still learn.

"It is," David Halberstam said, "a very, very satisfying life."

April 26, 2007

Court of Public Opinion

I once got a remarkable insight from former Mayor David Dinkins about prejudice in New York. I asked Dinkins whether white, Hispanic, and Asian New Yorkers were biased against him because he is black—a bias that sometimes seemed to be cloaked in criticism about his passion for playing tennis and attending tournaments.

"If I had gone to a basketball game, it would be all right," Dinkins retorted. Then he elaborated: "I think there's a bias against tennis. People don't understand that tennis is a wonderful sport. The king of Sweden played until he was eight-five."

The king of Sweden surely would have been a member of a language minority in America, but he probably never experienced racial prejudice as Dinkins had. Still, the mayor insisted, it was nothing personal. "I've said very clearly, people aren't biased against me because I like tennis," Dinkins explained. "I said they're biased against tennis."

Given the fact that nearly two decades have elapsed since then, I wondered whether prejudice still plays out the same way today. It's also two decades since a national columnist scoffed at Governor Mario Cuomo's chances of getting elected president by noting dismissively, "There are no Marios down South."

Just think, this year American voters are mulling a diverse field of presidential candidates that includes a black, a woman, a Mormon, a twice-divorced Italian American Catholic born in Brooklyn—and that's not even counting Mayor Bloomberg, who describes himself as a diminutive, divorced Jewish billionaire.

A survey by the Pew Research Center found that Americans were more likely to support a presidential candidate who is gay, Muslim, who's taken antidepressants, or has cheated on a spouse than one who doesn't believe in God.

The Pew sample was too small to compare whether New Yorkers share the same prejudices as other Americans. But, luckily, Zogby International released a survey, timed to the GSN television series *Without Prejudice?*, on the same subject.

John Zogby himself acknowledges that people tend to lie—that is, to give "socially acceptable" responses—when asked about their views on race. He tried to overcome that by asking instead what they think "most Americans" believe. What they believe, according to the poll, is that most Americans are biased against minority groups.

What about New Yorkers? Like other Americans, they're more likely to rule out supporting a woman for president than a black. They're also more likely to rule out a candidate who's older than seventy . . . but less likely to rule out a gay candidate or an atheist.

Shown pictures of ordinary people, New Yorkers were less likely to trust white men, young or older, and more likely to trust a bespectacled white woman of a certain age.

They're less likely than other Americans to want to work with a deaf person. Less likely to say that extremely religious people are inherently moral. More likely to blame men for global warming and Republicans for poverty. New Yorkers are more likely to tolerate their children's dating people from other religions—except Mormons. And a little more likely to associate blacks with crime.

While we're supersensitive these days about most slurs, Andrew Sullivan once argued in the *New York Times Magazine* that verbal expressions of prejudice serve a useful social purpose—letting off steam. "Anyone who has lived in the ethnic shouting match that is New York City knows exactly what I mean," he wrote. "If New Yorkers disliked each other less, they wouldn't be able to get on so well."

In 1989, the year David Dinkins was elected the city's first black mayor, nine of the candidates actually signed a pledge to avoid appeals to prejudice based on race, ethnicity, national identity, sex, or sexual orientation—although they didn't necessarily agree on just what constituted such an appeal.

Next year, with the presidential field so incredibly New York–centric, the bigger political question may not be about the biases of New Yorkers as much as whether the rest of America is prejudiced against New York.

No New Yorker has been nominated on a national ticket by a major party since Jack Kemp of Buffalo ran for vice president in 1996. None has been elected since FDR in 1944—unless you count Richard Nixon, who voted for himself in California in 1968 with an absentee ballot from New York.

Neither the Pew nor the Zogby polls gauged the nation's attitudes toward New York, although the city happens to be home, disproportionately, to many of the groups Americans are biased against.

Nor did either poll attempt to measure another controversial question: whether most people really do have anything against tennis.

July 26, 2007

In 2016, Donald J. Trump of Queens, New York, was elected president, defeating Hillary Rodham Clinton of Chappaqua, New York.

The Mayor's Man

"**N**ew York is the greatest city in the world—and everything is wrong with it."

Those words were the opening salvo of the *Herald Tribune*'s award-winning "City in Crisis" series in 1965. Under Dick Schaap's direction, Barry Gottehrer and his reporting team drafted a damning indictment of the years of official smugness they blamed for New York's spiraling descent.

They coupled blame with a promising urban manifesto—a platform that would transform a patrician Manhattan congressman, John V. Lindsay, into a pre-Giuliani version of "America's Mayor."

When I heard that Barry Gottehrer was gravely ill, I envisioned him back in 1965. He was barely thirty then. More mature than some of his fellow crusaders, but very much the fresh face that, as Murray Kempton wrote, John Lindsay projected and attracted . . . when everyone else in politics was tired.

Beginners, Gottehrer called them. They still brashly harbored illusions about what was possible in government.

"Remember those good old days in New York City," Gottehrer said much later, "when we all were young, beautiful, invincible and we all really cared."

But in the end, he concluded, "the more honest you are with yourself, the more you realize that the best kind of power, your power for constructive change, is very limited."

Lindsay had promised "change and reform and progress." Maybe two out of three wasn't so bad.

Today we justly congratulate ourselves that good policing has helped reduce crime to the lowest levels since the 1960s. New Yorkers weren't so sanguine then, though. Cops were engaged in what one former police commissioner acknowledged was "a war that seemingly had no end."

In Gottehrer's "City in Crisis," the gulf between rich and poor was growing. The Fiscal Policy Institute says it's still widening.

In 1965, more than 70,000 young people were out of work and out of school. Now, by one measure, twice as many are.

But with all its vulnerabilities and imperfections, New York today is not a chaotic city in crisis.

Back then, everybody was revolting, even the Mafia. Negotiating over the site of an Italian unity rally, associates of Joe Colombo demanded that several venerable trees in Central Park be removed because they blocked the stage. "Don't worry," one Colombo man assured Gottehrer. "I'll send some boys around late tonight. They'll take care of it. Nobody will miss a thing."

Gottehrer vetoed the attempted arborcide. But he was vilified more than once for consorting with organized-crime figures, for courting and coddling racists. Whatever the excesses of the enduring costs of defusing the crises Lindsay inherited and provoked, though, Gottehrer's unconventional tactics helped keep New York cool during the proverbial long, hot summers when other cities burned.

He described himself as a "white in a world of black and brown, a moderate in a world of revolutionaries, trying to bring change where change seemed needed most, trying to buy time until the change would come."

Nick Pileggi wrote in the *Times Magazine* that Lindsay's presidential prospects might depend on this "consciously inconspicuous" assistant whom Pileggi described as "short, unpretentious . . . in a sports shirt and slouch . . . deep, sad, dark eyes. . . . The whole contour of his face projects such uncontentious melancholy that many of his battles—and potentially Mayor Lindsay's—are de-escalated with a wan smile and a handshake."

The Bronx-born Gottehrer, Pileggi wrote, was charged with "orchestrating municipal chaos—dealing in the process with well-meaning clergymen, jealous community leaders, poverty-fund rivals, police-precinct captains, sniping political contenders, merchant groups, machete-carrying militants, aggressive peace demonstrators, law-and-order radicals and incipient rioters—into a cacophonous truce."

The bold vision and bromides of the urban agenda weren't his department. He dispensed quick fixes.

But the crusade he had helped launch and then joined was being numbed by perpetual crises, by its own self-justifying version of incumbency's inevitable official smugness. Gottehrer, himself, became expendable.

"I gave myself pep talks more frequently," he said, "that were based less on our achievements than on the belief that other administrations, on the whole, did a lot worse."

When he left city government, Gottehrer got a personal pep talk from Marvin Schick, a fellow mayoral assistant:

"Your achievements are not glossy, for the material that you have had to work with is not the glamorous side of society," Schick wrote in a parting appreciation. "But also for this reason, your achievements are real and alive and will continue to bear good fruit long after you have spent your last day at City Hall. I know of no more glorious way to leave the public employ."

April 12, 2007

This podcast was posted on April 10, 2008, at nytimes.com and iTunes. Barry Gottehrer heard it from his hospital bed. He died the next day.

New York's Wild West Side

If Zane Grey means anything to New Yorkers these days, his name most likely conjures up glorious images of the Old West. Beginning a century ago, Grey wrote dozens of novels that defined and popularized Western folklore and cowboy culture—rugged, independent, sensitive, but still more Marlboro Man than *Brokeback Mountain*.

When he died in 1939, the *New York Times* editorialized that Grey had succeeded in getting Easterners to "swallow the Western legend."

What most people don't know, though, is that before Zane Grey reinvented himself as a writer of the purple sage, he was a dentist in Manhattan.

And before he embraced Horace Greeley's dictum and went west in 1907 on a trip to trap mountain lions, he could be found dodging a much wilder species—one with horns and a trunk—on Manhattan's West Side.

Why do I know this?

Because as a kid growing up in Brooklyn, I devoured Grey's books, and as we approach the centennial of his first successful novel, I've been mulling writing about him.

And how do I know this?

Because of the miracle of digitization, which enabled me to stumble upon an obscure reference to him in a *Times* newspaper story in 1902.

Well, good for me, but why should anyone else care?

The answer is, because I discovered that the fabled Code of the West— those unwritten rules of the trail that readers gleaned from Zane Grey's horse operas—may have originated no farther west than Columbus Avenue in Manhattan, literally, as rules of the road.

In recent years, Grey's idealized code has been reissued in writing by local governments in western states as a more or less official liability disclaimer and warning to city slickers. These Codes of the New West are explicit caveats to prospective newcomers against the sort of expectations reflexively assumed as a right by entitled New Yorkers—dare I say, West Siders, in particular.

For example, forget about calling the police, the fire department, or an ambulance and expecting them to respond promptly.

Don't complain about unpaved roads—yes, they generate unpleasant dust, but get over it—and don't expect neighbors to join in petitioning for improved services.

Don't assume you own the water running through your property or the minerals beneath it.

Don't gripe about farmers who use noisy machines at night.

Don't build your house on the highest hilltop—it's more vulnerable to the elements, and you ruin everyone else's view.

And, as the code of Gallatin County, Montana, warns, "Animal manure can and often does cause 'objectionable' odors. What else can we say? No whining!"

Like the latest version, Grey's code of coexistence was designed to reconcile old-timers and newcomers. One axiom was, in so many words, mind your own business. That's because many migrants went west not only to find their fortune but also to avoid bill collectors and other *nudnicks* back home. They reinvented themselves.

Grey did, too, but before he even got there.

For reasons that seem self-evident, he dropped his first name: Pearl. For reasons that remain less obvious, he changed the spelling of *Gray* to the British version, with an *e*.

After graduating from the University of Pennsylvania in 1896, Grey reluctantly followed in his father's professional footsteps. He became a dentist, moved to New York City, and opened a practice on West 21st Street.

Grey lived at 100 West 74th Street, practically around the corner from the storied apartment house that was named the Dakota when it opened less than two decades earlier—supposedly because the sparsely populated neighborhood evoked the barren western territory that had not yet achieved statehood.

He played semi-pro baseball in New Jersey. He fished on the Delaware

River. When the journal *Recreation* published his article about fishing in 1903, he was hooked as a wordsmith.

He spent one winter writing a novel by gaslight in the kitchen of his dingy apartment. It was about a distant ancestor who helped fend off attacks from the British and Indians on an Ohio frontier fort. A New York book editor dismissively advised Grey to stick with his day job, but he abandoned dentistry altogether. His first commercial success was a full-fledged Western inspired by his mountain lion expedition.

The same year his fishing yarn was published, Grey's name also appeared in the *New York Times*.

The city's Board of Aldermen was considering raising the legal speed limit for bicycles and motor vehicles—from eight miles per hour to ten, which happens to be more than twice as fast as a crosstown bus travels in rush hour today.

Safety-conscious citizens protested the increase. They commissioned a postcard poll. Among the 6,000 New Yorkers who responded—along with John D. Rockefeller Jr. and Felix Adler, founder of the Ethical Culture Society—was Dr. Zane Grey of West 74th Street.

More government regulation might not have been consistent with the Code of the West that Grey would help promulgate, but his comments to the pollsters evinced just the kind of rugged individualism that he would champion.

"I was nearly killed by an auto yesterday," Grey wrote, "and hereafter I shall carry a gun. Nothing but a bullet could have caught this one!"

May 10, 2007

Dynasty

Polly Noonan once dismissed her role as merely "a full-time grandmother."

"I have no power," she insisted.

Noonan died in 2003. Last week, her granddaughter Kirsten Gillibrand was appointed to fill Hillary Rodham Clinton's unexpired term in the U.S. Senate. Gillibrand, an upstate New York Democratic congresswoman, called her grandmother "my greatest political hero."

A lot was made over the fact that in getting appointed by Governor Paterson to the Senate seat, Gillibrand had edged out the scions of two political dynasties, Andrew Cuomo and Caroline Kennedy. But less was said about her own pedigree and her grandmother's roots in Dan O'Connell's legendary Albany Democratic machine.

In 1940, O'Connell installed Erastus Corning II, the patrician great-grandson of the founder of the New York Central Railroad, as mayor. He would serve forty-two years, until his death in 1983.

Polly Noonan's association with Corning started earlier, in the 1930s. She was his secretary in the state Senate. She would become what was described as his closest confidant. Polly's daughter (Kirsten Gillibrand's mother) was Mayor Corning's goddaughter. A half-dozen other Noonan relatives worked for the city or county.

"Dan O'Connell was the nominal leader," recalls Mario Cuomo, who clerked at the Court of Appeals in the late 1950s. "Corning was the *de facto* leader. Polly *was* the leader."

Under Governor Cuomo, she was also vice chairwoman of the Democratic State Committee. For more than thirty years, and until the day she died, she was president of the Albany County Democratic Women.

Her early views on womens' lib were elemental. She was once accused of punching the wife of a rebellious ward leader in the ribs. She didn't mince words, either. As a Senate staffer, she recalled, "I'd tell our Democratic members, if they wanted to put their girlfriend on the payroll, fine, but only do it after a Republican senator puts his girlfriend on the payroll. Then each one has someone on the other."

Defending the Democratic organization against charges of bossism, she declared, "There's no machine. There never was a machine, because Erastus Corning and Dan O'Connell cared about the people. A machine doesn't have a heart—our organization did."

As to her own heart, rumors abounded about her relationship with Corning (who, by the way, delighted in spooking visitors by displaying his collection of animal penises). Regardless of whether a romance was ever consummated—and Paul Grondahl's exhaustive biography of the mayor is inconclusive—Noonan and Corning could not have been closer.

"Their lives," Grondahl wrote, "remained inextricably linked through politics and personal devotion."

The Albany author William Kennedy told me that Noonan "was always known as the 'confidant' of Erastus, and all power derived from that."

At Corning's funeral in 1983, Kennedy recalled in his book *O Albany!*, the mayor's relatives tried to keep that link private. "Some TV newsmen," Kennedy wrote, "were asked not to focus undue attention on Polly Noonan."

But how could they help it? Corning, in effect, disinherited his wife and children. He left the Noonan family his insurance business, which generously sold coverage to anyone who wanted to do business with the government. Corning survivors sued to overturn the will; they lost.

Polly's daughter married Doug Rutnik. Rutnik was Corning's surrogate son and hunting buddy. The couple has since divorced. He's now a lobbyist who's represented Morgan Stanley and Lockheed Martin—both of which have won state contracts. He's also a close associate of former Senator Alfonse D'Amato.

D'Amato is a Republican, but no matter. In incestuous Albany, Gillibrand was a college intern in D'Amato's office. Her father dated Zenia Mucha, a former strategist for D'Amato and later for Governor George Pataki.

Meanwhile, D'Amato, a lobbyist himself now, has been cozying up to David Paterson, the Democratic governor who appointed Gillibrand.

Paterson's Republican challenger next year might be Rudy Giuliani, D'Amato's nemesis.

In New York, all politics is personal.

"As a ten-year-old girl, I would listen to my grandmother discuss issues, and she made a lasting impression on me," Senator Gillibrand has said. "What I admired so much about her was her passion. I thought, 'Someday I may serve, someday I may be part of this.'"

January 29, 2009

Hymie, We Hardly Knew Ye

That this is twenty-nine-year-old Marissa Shorenstein's fifth Democratic national convention only begins to hint at her family's political longevity. Her great-great-uncle Hymie Shorenstein, the legendary party boss of Brownsville, Brooklyn, was a delegate to the raucous Democratic National Convention in New York in 1924.

He suffered a slight concussion at that convention but survived to spawn a political dynasty that includes Marissa's father, Stuart, a Manhattan lawyer who served recently as a Democratic district leader on the West Side of Manhattan; her mother, Janice, who ran for the City Council in 1989, when Marissa was nine; and Walter Shorenstein, a first cousin, twice removed, the California real estate mogul and major Democratic contributor, who also endowed Harvard's Joan Shorenstein Center on the Press, Politics and Public Policy, named for his daughter, a *CBS News* producer.

"It's genetic," said Marissa Shorenstein, who majored in government at Harvard, then worked for Democratic candidates nationally and in New York and now serves as Governor David A. Paterson's deputy communications director.

Years before controversies over multilingualism and English as the nation's official language, before New York had a governor who is legally blind and cannot read, Hymie Shorenstein served as Brooklyn's commissioner of records. A rival's challenge to his literacy in 1933 produced this famous exchange:

"Can you read or write English?" Hymie was asked.

"That's my personal business," he replied.

"Don't you think a Commissioner of Records should be able to read and write?"

"What difference does it make?"

"Did you go to school?"

"I had no time. I came here when I was ten and led a horse around for a factory. I had to support my mother. I joined the party when I was eighteen—no, change that, make it twenty-one."

Not surprisingly, the court concluded that the duties of the commissioner of records were not enumerated and that "inability to read or write does not render the commissioner an unsuitable person within the meaning of the statute." The court ruled that Hymie had served effectively as a marshal during the war "when the post required tact, intelligence, resourcefulness and unusual diligence," and that as a director of an investment company and of the Brooklyn National Bank, he had been vetted by federal and state authorities.

"Some of our best businessmen cannot read nor write," the judge noted. Hymie held the job for another decade, until the La Guardia administration abolished it.

His influence extended well beyond the blurry borders of the neighborhood in which he would spend most of his life—he often disputed its reputation as a breeding ground for violent crime, even complaining that "one would think that Brownsville was to Brooklyn what Cicero was to Chicago"—and even of Brooklyn.

As a delegate to the 1924 Democratic National Convention in Manhattan, he managed to be singled out for a degree of notoriety—an achievement in itself at a convention punctuated by 103 roll calls before a presidential candidate was finally nominated. During the sixty-eighth roll call, while he was rallying Al Smith supporters in the Pennsylvania delegation, the rotund, mustachioed Hymie was struck by the head of Senator Thomas Walsh's mahogany gavel as the convention chairman vigorously attempted to restore order on the floor of Madison Square Garden.

In 1928, he would claim credit for Smith's nomination at that year's convention, which was held in Houston—to appease the Protestant, prohibitionist South, which had not hosted a national convention since the Civil War and was hostile to a nominee who was not only from New York but a Catholic. He was credited with quelling an eleventh-hour revolt in the Ohio delegation, assuring Smith's nomination.

The story is told about one worried candidate who confronted Hymie on Election Day, seeking reassurances that he would win. Hymie reminded the man of the ferries that plied the harbor, inevitably trailed by a field of flotsam.

"Not to worry," Hymie famously told the anxious candidate. Roosevelt (or Smith, depending on the version) is the ferry boat; "You are the garbage."

September 4, 2008

Nowhere to Go But Up

If you're crawling crosstown more slowly than New Yorkers did one hundred years ago . . .

Or watching helplessly as another jam-packed bus passes you by . . .

Or waiting on an endless line for a cup of coffee . . .

Then you must be wondering: Just how much more crowded can New York City get?

Well, so did I. So I asked the kind of experts who come to the phone when the *Times* calls.

Their answer is: a lot more crowded.

New Yorkers are confronting a phenomenon that few other cities in the Northeast or Midwest now face: a growing population.

Frankly, elected officials are typically consumed with the present. They're rarely concerned about the past. And they almost never have the resources or motivation to engage in long-range planning, particularly for growth. That's going to be somebody else's problem.

In the mid-1970s a short-lived proposal for "planned shrinkage" was advanced, sandwiched between a 1969 look at the challenges facing the city along with some ambitious solutions, and another candid but largely optimistic assessment in 1987.

This time, Mayor Bloomberg promises a plan by the spring. And the planning is starting none too soon. For New York's 400th birthday party in 2025, the city might need an extra million or so slices of cake.

New York has ranked first in population among American cities since the first census in 1790. But since the 1940s, more people have been leaving the city for other parts of the country than arriving from out of town. Growth in the 1980s and especially the 1990s has been driven largely by immigration from overseas.

Today the population is officially 8.2 million.

Immigrants keep coming, and with Hispanic and Asian New Yorkers continuing to have higher birthrates, the population is projected to pass 9 million by 2020 and 9.4 million by 2025.

Where are we going to put all those people? Where are they going to live? Where are they going to work? Where are their kids going to go to school? Where are we going to send their garbage?

Fifty years ago, when TV antennas were beginning to sprout on rooftops and the alternate-side parking minuet was just being choreographed, the biggest concern of planners in the nation's biggest city was that we would run out of space. And that's when New York still counted 268 farms—farms that together would have equaled one-and-a-half Central Parks.

One story in the *Times* back then predicted that with less and less unused space for housing, "[T]he end now seems not too far—somewhere around 1975, or, at most optimistic measures, the year 2000."

Just three years ago, the only vestige of the last privately owned, commercial working farm in the city, two acres in Fresh Meadows, Queens, was finally sold to a developer for $4.3 million.

Well, a lot has changed in fifty years, but we haven't run out of space. Instead, we keep recycling it.

We haven't run out of jobs, either.

Fifty years ago, the census still found 2,000 telegraph messengers and 600 blacksmiths. It found one today. Also fewer TV repairmen.

But there are more parking attendants, security guards, auto mechanics, and cabbies. Also, more doctors, real estate agents, designers, and social workers.

A half-century ago, nearly three in ten New Yorkers were employed in manufacturing, more than in any other industry classification. Today, fewer than one in ten is. But for the first time since World War II, manufacturing jobs, not counting the apparel industry, have not declined.

The questions city officials are grappling with now are:

How big can we grow?

How big do we want to grow?

And how can we best plan to accommodate that growth?

Growth for its own sake isn't necessarily good. But as Deputy Mayor Dan Doctoroff says, "It opens up great opportunities if the growth is smart . . . if we have the things that make cities worth living in."

February 19, 2006

Projections proved a bit optimistic, or pessimistic, depending on your views about density. By 2018, the population passed a record 8.6 million, and growing.

History Lessons

Lost and Founded

The other day, while working on an article about the founding of New York City, I had a sobering revelation. New York is almost 400 years old. Which means I've now been covering the city for more than 10 percent of its existence.

Maybe you're wondering: Why, after reporting for forty years, am I just now catching up on something as fundamental as when the city was founded?

Better late than never, I guess.

You also might be thinking, after forty years, can't this guy find anything more significant to write about?

Also a good question. But sometimes even the smallest details offer the most vivid insights into how government works. That turned out to be true again in this case. Even a fact as seemingly inviolable as the date of the city's founding can be subject to political manipulation and bureaucratic bungling.

The city's official seal is itself a crazy quilt of historical incongruities.

Flanking the shield are the sailor, named Dexter, and the Indian, called Sinister (the names, ostensibly, denoting their positions). There are two beavers, symbols of the garment center's earlier origins and a talisman of New York's distinct commercial roots. There are the flour barrels, reminding us of the city's early monopoly on milling, and also, by extension, of making dough.

An American eagle replaced the royal crown on an early version of the seal. The Dutch windmill remained. At the beginning of the twentieth century, in another bow to the political and cultural clout of the garment industry, the city fathers hemmed Dexter the Sailor's long pants. They also changed the date on the seal from 1686, when the British governor granted a charter from the king, to 1664. That's the year when the city's residents, fed up with the cavalier government of Peter Stuyvesant, all but invited the British to seize New Amsterdam from the Dutch and rename it New York.

Preoccupied by two world wars and the Depression, the city left the seal alone until the mid-1970s. The mayor then was Abe Beame, who happened to have been born in England but was by no means an Anglophile. The City Council president was the Irish-born Paul O'Dwyer, who, if not an Anglophobe, was surely no fan of the British government.

O'Dwyer was one of the dwindling number of New Yorkers who, every November, still celebrated Evacuation Day, which marked the ignominious British withdrawal from the city after the American Revolution. Yet every day, walking into City Hall, O'Dwyer would be confronted by 1664 on the official flag and seal—a galling reminder of British hegemony.

And if he needed another reason, what better time to change the date, to restore the Dutch to their proper historical pedestal, than on the 700th birthday of Amsterdam?

Whatever O'Dywer's motivation, he was suddenly confronted by a big problem. If not 1664, when?

The year 1624 seemed the most plausible alternative, but most of the people who arrived then were Walloons, from what would become Belgium. So much for the pretext of honoring the Dutch.

Sixteen-twenty-six? That's when New York established itself as the nation's real estate capital with that legendary $24 bargain between Peter Minuit and the Indians. But did we really want to rub that deal in the noses of Native Americans? And no deed was ever found.

So the City Council split the difference. It settled on 1625—a year in which perhaps the most visible event was when the settlers on what is now Governors Island moved their cattle to Lower Manhattan. (Foraging was better there because the Indians had cleared it for cultivation.)

Tinkering with the date created other problems. One piece of legislation, in describing the seal, forgot to mention one of the two beavers. Another attempt by O'Dwyer to obliterate any British vestige removed from the flag—but not from the seal—the legend, which included the Latin name for York, in England.

Today the consensus among historians is that the Council made a mistake.

July 17, 2008

The Summer of Sam

Where were you when the lights went out?

I remember where I was. On the beach in Nantucket. Furious.

Here it was, the biggest story of the summer, maybe the year, and I was out of town.

I rushed back only to realize that the blackout was only part of the story. The summer of 1977 was when New York went nuts. Many New Yorkers might not remember. In fact, nearly half the people living in the city today weren't even born then.

But talk about long hot summers.

A mountain climber from Queens named George Willig scaled the World Trade Center. Terrorist bombs linked to Puerto Rican nationalists exploded at Manhattan office buildings and department stores. The temperature—not the real feel—hit 104 degrees, nearly breaking the record high. Elvis Presley died. Studio 54 opened, The Bronx's most dysfunctional family, the Yankees, revived their legendary World Series rivalry against the Dodgers. Abe Beame was struggling to avoid being the first elected mayor in more than half a century to be defeated for a second term. A psychopathic serial killer armed with a forty-four-caliber revolver and dubbed Son of Sam held New York hostage as no crime figure had done in the decades since a disgruntled former Consolidated Edison worker, George Metesky, periodically vented his rage as the folkloric Mad Bomber.

And, oh yes, a Con Ed blackout that July triggered looting that resulted in more than 3,000 arrests.

All those goings-on were too much for one season, so the metaphorical summer of 1977 lasted seven months. It begin in March and ended in October, and it fell more or less at the midway point of a demi-decade when New Yorkers were desperately grasping at competing visions of where their city was going.

One vision concluded that the good old days were behind it, that since the 1950s the city had passed its prime and grown unmanageable.

The other vision defined New York as a resilient immigrant Mecca where, once the neglected crater-size potholes and social pockmarks were repaired, the streets would again be paved with gold.

Today we know which vision would prevail . . . but, believe me, nobody did back then.

If you want to relive it from the comfort of your living room, you can watch the series on ESPN or, better yet, rent a video of Spike Lee's *Summer of Sam*. Jimmy Breslin introduced the film, standing in squeaky-clean Times Square and inviting the audience to travel back in time.

"This film is about a different time," he deadpanned, "a different place, the good old days, the hot, blistering summer of 1977."

Breslin was being ironic about the good old days, of course. That extended summer of 1977 was an anarchic epoch. It was shaped, anomalously, by two mostly disparate forces: bankers and bond raters, who had profited from the city's debt but had finally decided to punish New Yorkers for being too profligate; and by the last gasps of an anything-goes sexual revolution still raging at jammed Manhattan discos while the biggest police manhunt in the city's history was emptying isolated lovers' lanes in Brooklyn and Queens.

You could argue that 1977 wasn't New York's worst year.

Think 1990, when New Yorkers worried that Mayor Ed Koch's early success in recovering from the city's fiscal crisis was an aberration, or whether, in fact, the naysayers of 1977 were right, that New York was ungovernable. That year, the murder toll set a record, when the city was building more jail cells than apartments. A film released that year titled *King of New York* proclaimed, "Not everyone who runs a city is elected." It was about a drug kingpin.

Remember more recently, 2001, when the city was attacked by terrorists, when nearly 3,000 people were killed—not merely arrested—and when the city's skyline and its psyche suffered permanent scars.

Still, that summer three decades ago epitomized New York at its nuttiest. And while it wouldn't end until October—when the Bronx was burning, but the Yankees won the World Series—New Yorkers were able to breathe easier briefly a few weeks after the big blackout because the police captured the forty-four-caliber killer and ended a months-long terror spree during which he taunted the police and the press with bizarre handwritten notes. He worked as a mail sorter, giving new definition to the term "going postal." Jimmy Breslin said of David Berkowitz: the first murderer he knew of who understood how to wield a revolver and a semicolon. And in one of those "only in New York" episodes, he was caught because at the scene of his final stake-out, he was illegally parked and got a ticket.

The night he was captured—after police remembered to get a search warrant and some of the other formalities that might have been overlooked—at police headquarters Mayor Beame barely avoided the photo op from hell, when he mistook Berkowitz for a cop and almost shook hands to congratulate him on great detective work.

The next morning, my wife was taking a taxi to work when the radio announced the arrest. The driver, still reeling from the uncertainties of the city's fiscal crisis, was perplexed. Why, he asked, would anyone jeopardize a civil service job to become a serial killer?

July 12, 2007

In 2003, only two years after the 9/11 terrorist attack, New York was again plunged into darkness. But this blackout, which struck much of the Northeast and Midwest, prompted mostly frustration, humor, and stubborn resilience.

The Little Steamboat That Could

New Yorkers don't know much, or care much, about our history. We're a little concerned about our future, but mostly preoccupied by the present.

Which is why, I guess, it's not a surprise that the 200th anniversary of a signal event in establishing the city's preeminence is about to pass barely noticed, much less suitably commemorated.

It took place on August 17, 1807, not far from Ground Zero in Lower Manhattan and the Paulus Hook ferry to Jersey City and near where the Greenwich State Prison once stood.

The crowd of New Yorkers that had gathered there were skeptical—even then. Their cynicism was redeemed. After the ceremonial tooting of a tin horn, followed by some muscular whirring and creaking and hissing and churning, nothing happened.

But, finally, after another toot, the bright vermillion paddle wheels began turning, splashing unsuspecting passengers and spectators, and a new era of steamboat navigation was inaugurated.

Depending on the winds and tides, sailing vessels could easily take four days to make the 150-mile journey to Albany. Robert Fulton's little steamboat arrived in 30 hours.

So far-fetched did his feat seem at the time that when he returned to New York City on August 21, the skeptics demanded sworn affidavits that he had been to Albany and back. Other boat owners took him seriously, though. They were so worried about the competition that Fulton's ferry was occasionally the target of sabotage—which may be why a harpoon gun was mounted on its bow.

Fulton's successful, commercially viable commute helped establish New York as a gateway to the rest of the nation.

His innovation and perseverance was another example of good old American know-how—perfecting the advances of earlier inventors and then capitalizing on political influence. He persuaded the Albany lawmakers to guarantee his investment by granting him and his patron, Robert Livingston, a monopoly on river navigation by steam.

In the Hudson Valley, the state historic site in Clermont, where Livingston lived, has scheduled a number of anniversary programs this summer. But don't hold your breath for a celebration here rivaling the centennial in 1907. That August, virtually every boat in the harbor blew its horn or whistle to salute Fulton, the artist-turned-inventor who also designed a submarine that he hoped would deter war. A giant peace flag, the world's largest, was unfurled from the Singer Building in Manhattan, which was then the world's tallest.

Perhaps assuming that New Yorkers could take only so much history, the Fulton centennial was combined with the tercentenary two years later, in 1909, of Henry Hudson's famous exploration of what would become his eponymous river. Actually, it would be known every where else as the Hudson except in New York. Here, well past the early twentieth century, it would still be called the North River, to distinguish it from the Delaware, which the Dutch had named the South. Fulton's steamboat was also known early on as the *North River* but was later christened the *Clermont*.

In 1909, Stephen Chalmers, a *Times* reporter, drolly looked ahead to what New York would be like in 2009, when a Hudson–Fulton celebration of sorts is scheduled to be held, too. Chalmers predicted the development of wireless color photography, the triumph of air travel—buildings would be built up or leveled off at 1,000 feet tall so planes could land on them—and even a race to Chicago and back by competing pilots from Hoboken and from Mars.

He made another forecast, too, which suggests that we're not much better at predicting the future than at celebrating the past.

Chalmers didn't know then, of course, about Mayor Bloomberg's congestion-pricing plan to reduce automobile traffic. But by 2009, he wrote, the automobile—still brand new in 1909—would be obsolete. New York's streets, he predicted, would be reserved exclusively for pedestrians.

August 9, 2007

Work Is a Four-Letter Word

One of the most memorable moments in the history of New York City's labor movement was when Victor Gotbaum threatened to throw Albert Shanker out of a hotel room window.

That was three decades ago, and while I wasn't in the room, Gotbaum, who will be eighty-six next month, convincingly recounts the story in gory detail to this day.

Shanker, you may remember, was the teachers' union president—like Gotbaum, a towering and progressive figure in American labor. He was immortalized in Woody Allen's film *Sleeper*, in which the world as we know it was destroyed by atomic warfare. That war began, Allen was told after waking up Rip Van Winkle–style, when "a man named Albert Shanker got hold of a nuclear warhead."

The allusion was to school decentralization and the teachers' strikes in the late 1960s. But figuratively, at least, Shanker nearly destroyed a world as we knew it in 1975. Concerned that outside fiscal monitors would void recent contract gains, he balked at investing $150 million from the teachers' union pension fund in municipal securities—almost triggering New York City's bankruptcy. Governor Hugh Carey and an angry Gotbaum finally persuaded Shanker to relent.

With Labor Day barbecues and shopping almost upon us again, what an opportune time to reflect on how far the union movement has come since then.

Labor Day was a New York invention. The first parade in the city was held in 1882. The first state legislation to declare Labor Day an official holiday was introduced in Albany. In its earliest incarnations, the holiday was celebrated on a Saturday, then a Tuesday, which shows where labor stood in those days.

Labor Day officially began in New York 120 years ago.

An 1887 *Times* editorial immediately denounced the holiday as "a piece of class legislation of the most objectionable kind" and urged that it be repealed.

Instead, the national government followed suit, declaring the first Monday in September as Labor Day—in large part to foster a more respectable alternative to the radical and sometimes violent commemorations of May Day.

In the city's first Labor Day parades, placards denounced capitalists, championed an eight-hour workday, and even demanded rent-free housing, but red flags were barred.

For all the dogma about solidarity, organized labor was pretty disorganized then, too. The first formal parade was actually two parades. The building trades, always marching to their own drummer, went up Fifth Avenue from Grand Army Plaza. Everyone else—including cigar packers, pattern makers, lithographers, striking telegraph operators, and other workers mostly reflecting the city's manufacturing base—marched downtown.

Within ten years, labor leaders caught up with their constituents, agreeing that working people deserved a real day off instead of having to traipse around Union Square on a September Monday. Picnics replaced parades.

Samuel Gompers, that giant of American labor, objected. He could see what was coming. Department store sales would be next, further enriching the owners of retail emporiums spending their three-day weekend in the suburbs while forcing retail clerks to work.

"Labor Day without demonstrations, parades and meetings," he wrote in 1907, "will as sure as the sun rises and sets lose its distinctive characteristic and simply become a holiday for jollification, without other purpose, design or result."

This year, there will be no Labor Day parade in the city. Actually there hasn't been a Labor Day parade *on* Labor Day in New York for years.

Union leaders decided that their annual public flexing of labor muscle to politicians was less important than appealing to their own constituents, who preferred to play rather than march.

Moreover, labor had less muscle to show off.

By 1981, when Harry Van Arsdale still headed the city's once-vaunted Central Labor Council, it took him two months to get a permit from the Police Department to revive the parade for the first time in thirteen years.

In 2007, an off-year politically anyway, the parade will be replaced by a rally later in September to support health care protection for workers at Ground Zero.

Union members constitute 20 percent or more of the workforce these days in only three states: New York, Hawaii, and Alaska. But last year, the share of New York workers who are union members dipped below 25 percent for the first time since the Federal Bureau of Labor Statistics has kept count.

What of Gotbaum, Shanker, and the other labor lions of yesteryear? They've largely been succeeded by cubs. Randi Weingarten of the teachers' union is still a force to be reckoned with. But Dennis Rivera, of the powerful health care workers, has left town to help his national union organize.

Brian McLaughlin, the former head of the Central Labor Council, is under indictment for embezzlement. He was last spotted working as an electrician again for the first time in a quarter-century—this time making $46 an hour at an apartment house under construction on Manhattan's West Side.

"Like anyone else," he explained philosophically, "I'm back at work because I need to work."

August 23, 2007

What Drives Us

Think New York, and what rarely comes to mind is highways. More than half of the city's 3 million households don't even own a car. New Yorkers account for fully one in three mass transit riders in the entire country.

And forget about traffic. Subway and bus riders included, New Yorkers spend more time commuting than residents of any other big city. According to one recent survey, the average speed on the 34th Street crosstown bus in Manhattan is 3.4 miles per hour. You could crawl faster.

Still, as America, or the rest of America, celebrates the fiftieth anniversary of the Interstate Highway System, it's an opportune time to reflect—not on the sidewalks of New York, but on the streets. Today, nearly 2 million motor vehicles are registered in the city, where they ply nearly 6,400 miles of roadway.

Navigating them was never easy, for vehicles or pedestrians. As far back as the 1860s, the Police Department formed its Broadway Squad— imposing officers who were at least six feet tall. Their mission: to help pedestrians cross the city's main thoroughfare.

In 1895, an eight-miles-per-hour speed limit was imposed to curb speed demon bicyclists.

Four years later, at West 74th Street and Central Park West, a sixty-one-year-old real estate broker named Henry Bliss stepped off a streetcar and was struck by an automobile. When he died the next morning, he became the first recorded motor vehicle fatality in North America.

In 1916, the first traffic lights were installed. They were a novelty. In New York, the way they worked was novel, too. Red was easy—everybody stop. But amber meant that only north–south traffic could proceed. And green meant that only crosstown traffic was allowed. So traveling on an avenue, you could get a summons for running a green light. After eight years of ambiguity, the system was finally changed. Now the signals are universal. To everybody, amber means speed up.

Politicians had been talking about a national highway system since the Depression, but it was not until 1956 that President Eisenhower managed to get one funded.

Interstates produced benefits, of course, but they also destroyed neighborhoods and killed off a number of central cities. In New York, the collapse of the West Side Highway prompted a prolonged debate over highways versus mass transit. In that case, mass transit won.

But guess which state has more interstate highways than all the rest? It's New York: with 29 different routes that stretch 1,600 miles. In terms of mileage, that's only about half the length of all the interstates in Texas, however.

The oldest segments of the system predate designation as interstates. One of those is a portion of Grand Central Parkway in Queens. It opened in 1936 and was later incorporated into I-278.

While the rest of the country marks the golden anniversary of the interstates, 2006, more or less, is the centennial of what has been billed as the nation's first public limited-access highway. Guess where? The Bronx!

Just as the federal government got the interstate system built under the guise of national defense, the Bronx River Parkway began as an environmental project. The Bronx River was so polluted that it was even blamed for poisoning wildlife at the Bronx Zoo. Naturally, the first impulse was to pave it over. But a road running north into Westchester, flanked by parkland, was envisioned as the vehicle both to clean up the river and provide a northern route out of the city. The first fifteen-mile stretch was finally completed in 1925. Instead of a ribbon, officials cut a rope of evergreen.

Admittedly, not many roads drive people to poetry—today, many just seem to drive without rhyme or reason. James Applewhite wrote a poem called "Interstate Highway," which began with meditation on bored and irritated drivers. And John Steinbeck once wrote, "When we get these thruways across the whole country, it will be possible to drive from New York to California without seeing a single thing."

But the opening of the Bronx River Parkway inspired Georgia Fraser. She contributed an ode, and the *Times* published it. It read, in part:

> The little streams of old New York
> Are buried deep beneath its stone—
> Carried in pipes and aqueducts
> Dried up, forgotten and alone . . .
> And you wee river, here you are
> For all the crowding years to come,
> Safe-gathered into nature's arms
> Oblivious of our motor's hum.

Hmmmm.

July 6, 2006

Election Lore

Mike Royko was right. Years ago, he proposed that Chicago adopt the slogan *Ubi Est Mea*. It sounds more high-minded in Latin. The motto means "Where's mine?"

What Royko meant was that while most politics is local, it's all *personal*. Which helps explain why the governor of Illinois is accused of trying to peddle Barack Obama's Senate seat to the highest bidder.

And also why whoever Governor Paterson appoints to succeed Senator Hillary Rodham Clinton of New York won't have to run for reelection in 2009. Instead, if that appointee wants to keep the Senate seat, he or she will have to go before the voters in 2010 and run for reelection again in 2012.

It all goes back to Harry Truman's hatred of Tom Dewey.

A half-century may seem like a long time to perpetrate a grudge. But for all the focus on what's been going on in Illinois, that's how the political process typically works in New York.

Politics is personal.

Our election law is very complicated—my friend Jerry Goldfeder just wrote an entire book about it. It doesn't take too much reading between the lines to understand that democracy has historically taken a back seat to contradictory goals: leveraging the law to perpetuate incumbency.

I couldn't find evidence in the Truman archives. But Justin Feldman, a prominent Manhattan lawyer who was close to several of the president's confidants, swears this story is true.

It's 1950. Two years after barely losing to President Truman, Dewey decides not to run again for governor of New York. The Democrats are poised to finally recapture the governorship and sweep the state. But they need to generate the traditionally heavy Democratic vote in New York City. That's what had happened the year before, in 1949. An interim Republican senator, John Foster Dulles, lost to Herbert Lehman because of the big New York mayoral vote that reelected Bill O'Dwyer.

In 1950, though, there's no mayoral election. No problem.

"What," says Ed Flynn, the wily Democratic boss of the Bronx, "if O'Dwyer resigned?"

O'Dwyer was ailing, physically and politically. Flynn conferred with Truman—no fan of O'Dwyer's. But given the prospect of a Democratic sweep in New York state, Truman agreed to name the mayor ambassador to Mexico. Which, conveniently, meant a new mayor would have to be elected that November, the same time as the governor and senator.

To make this long story shorter, New York Democrats were divided. Dewey got back into the gubernatorial race and won a third term. The next year, Republicans introduced legislation that would bar a race for mayor of New York in any general election when state or national officials were being chosen, too. (Two-thousand-nine is a mayoral election year.)

Here's another fact for Senator Clinton's potential successors to consider: Interim Senate appointees haven't fared very well. Since 1960, governors have appointed some fifty interim senators. Two were named just last year. Of the thirty-eight who ran for election, only eighteen won. New York's most recent interim appointee, Charles Goodell, lost when he sought a full term in 1970.

Given the state's political and financial deficit, Governor Paterson might be tempted to do Illinois one better and just auction the Senate seat on eBay.

He also might be tempted to extricate himself from the scrum in Albany by selecting himself. But that record isn't encouraging, either. Over the past seventy-five years, nine governors have filled Senate vacancies by appointing themselves. Only one—Albert Chandler of Kentucky in 1939—ran and retained his seat. No wonder his nickname was Happy.

Speaking of "Where's mine?" Senator Clinton could do the state a favor by resigning her Senate seat before her confirmation as secretary of state. With at least seven other Democratic freshmen being sworn in on January 3, resigning early would give her successor more seniority.

Her spokesman says, "It would be presumptuous to assume confirmation before the full Senate actually takes up the matter."

After all, only a decade ago, William Weld quit as governor of Massachusetts to accept a job from President Clinton. But his fellow Republicans in the Senate failed to confirm him. The nomination, by the way, was to be ambassador to Mexico—following in the footsteps of Bill O'Dwyer.

December 11, 2008

Kirsten Gillibrand was appointed to fill Clinton's seat. She won a special election in 2010 and was reelected to her first full term in 2012.

Evacuation Day

We celebrated July 4 on a Wednesday this year, which meant that most of the stories about the run-up to Independence Day seemed to be about how inconsiderate it was of the Founding Fathers, with all their foresight, not to figure out some way to permanently enshrine a longer holiday weekend.

Few New Yorkers remember, though, that for nearly a century, July 4 was rivaled as a patriotic holiday in the city by November 25.

July 1776 was when independence was declared, and when George Washington ordered the Declaration read to his troops.

But it was more than seven years later—two years after the British surrendered at Yorktown and months after the peace treaty was signed in Paris—that the last Redcoats left, the last cannonball of the Revolution was lobbed at the new nation, and that independence was officially won.

That was November 25, 1783, in New York.

George Washington returned to the city triumphantly, riding downtown by horseback and bar-hopping from the Hudson Valley and Harlem, into a city devastated by years of enemy occupation.

November 25 became known not so much as the day Washington arrived but as the day the British, taking advantage of favorable tides, finally sailed away in defeat from the city they had seized from the Dutch nearly 120 years earlier.

For whatever reason, November 25 became known not as Emancipation Day—which, arguably, it was for New Yorkers—but as Evacuation Day, which it most certainly was for the British.

145

Most New Yorkers had evacuated years before, not long after independence was declared, when General Washington and his troops stealthily slipped out of Brooklyn, rallied briefly in Manhattan, and then salvaged the army to fight on.

In August 1776, the first cannonball of the war was lobbed from a British frigate at Lower Manhattan, where young Alexander Hamilton and fellow Columbia students—it was called King's College then—were positioning artillery. Legend has it that the first shot pierced the roof of Fraunces Tavern, which still stands downtown and where Washington would celebrate his return.

In 1783, the last shot of the war was defiantly fired by a British frigate at jeering New Yorkers as the British departed, but it fell short of its intended target, on Staten Island.

The British perpetrated one further act of defiance before they left. They fastened the Union Jack to a flagpole in Bowling Green, then greased the pole so the British colors could not be lowered.

According to legend, a young American sailor named Van Arsdale nailed cleats to the pole, climbed it, ripped down the British ensign, and replaced it with an American flag.

That ritual was repeated on Evacuation Day for decades.

But while Boston still celebrates its own Evacuation Day—which conveniently coincides with St. Patrick's Day—the holiday spirit waned in New York. The annual parade of troops petered out during the Civil War, when most New Yorkers weren't feeling particularly celebratory. Then November 25 was subsumed by Thanksgiving. By World War I, the anti-British fervor stoked by Irish immigrants had also largely subsided.

In 1883, President Chester A. Arthur attended the Evacuation Day centennial, and the celebration was still ranked as "one of the great civic events of the nineteenth century in New York City." But by the turn of the century, the crumbs of what had been a patriotic feast were being fought over by competing veterans' groups.

Parks Commission president George Clausen, a German-American brewery owner, sided against a Van Arsdale descendant, Christopher Forbes, who had raised the flag at earlier ceremonies. To which Forbes sneered in a proverbial "so's your old man" rejoinder: "When my great-grandfather hauled down the British flag and hoisted the American colors I'd like to know where Mr. Clausen's great-grandfather was and what he was doing."

So, whatever you do on July 4, come next November remember that after independence was declared, hundreds of battles—nearly a third of them in New York state—were fought to achieve it.

And even if you're not Irish, don't forget Washington's fervent hope that Evacuation Day would "be remembered with admiration and applause to the last posterity."

Today there's a flagpole at Bowling Green. The most prominent feature in the park, near Wall Street, though, while also a reminder of New York's resiliency, is probably not the symbol that Washington had in mind. It's a bronze statue of a charging bull.

July 5, 2007

The First Thanksgiving

Maybe you missed it, but November 25 was Evacuation Day in New York. That's not just another name for the rush out of town before Thanksgiving. It's the anniversary of the day in 1783 when the last British troops finally left—ending their seven-year occupation, more than two years after they surrendered at Yorktown.

Perpetuated by descendants of patriots and Irish immigrants, Evacuation Day used to be bigger than Independence Day in New York. In truth, though, it's been celebrated even longer in Boston (thanks to cannons captured from the British at Fort Ticonderoga in upstate New York and aimed at the British fleet in Boston Harbor. The Redcoats evacuated Boston in 1776—sparing the city and escaping to Nova Scotia).

Which circuitously brings us to Thanksgiving. Was the original one really in Plymouth, Massachusetts, in 1621? Or was Thanksgiving actually inspired by events in Lower Manhattan seven years earlier?

Let's face it: New York has been shortchanged by history. That's partly our fault. New Yorkers were never much consumed with the past. We focus on the present and the short-term future. Like, tomorrow.

Look at Jamestown, Virginia. Jamestown bills itself as the nation's birthplace. Last year, it marked the 400th anniversary of the founding of the first permanent English colony. According to the official account, the colonists came ashore in 1607 never to leave. Except, they left.

America's beginnings can be more legitimately traced to New York, and just two years later. This January begins the 400th anniversary of Henry Hudson's voyage of discovery. As Ken Jackson, the Columbia University historian, said, "In Jamestown, they discover a town that disappears into the mud. New York becomes the greatest city in the world. The Hudson becomes the river west, the river of empire."

Sure, the Thanksgiving connection is a little more tenuous, but here goes:

First, consider the holiday a moveable feast. It was proclaimed by President Washington in 1789 in New York, when this city was still the nation's capital. Lincoln codified it as the last Thursday in November. Hoping to jump-start the economy by stretching the holiday shopping season during the Depression, Franklin Roosevelt moved it temporarily to the third Thursday.

FDR had a point: Do more Americans give thanks this week or go shopping? Which city most sanctifies commerce? For God's sake, some New Yorkers even call it the "Macy's Day Parade."

Massachusetts may boast more bogs than New York, but it's not number one in cranberry production. New York, meanwhile, produces 100 million pounds of pumpkins. And, anyway, devout Pilgrims were more into fasting than feasting.

But I digress. In November 1613, well before the Pilgrims, the Dutch navigator Adriaen Block sailed into New York harbor. He moored in an inlet near where the World Financial Center now stands. To make a long story short—and the details are pretty sketchy, anyway—the ship burned. According to some accounts, his crew constructed a few huts at what's now Broadway and Exchange Place. And with the help of Native Americans, they survived the winter and built a new ship.

They must have eaten. They might have invited the natives. They probably gave thanks.

"They have become an almost unknown footnote to very early American history," says Arthur Piccolo, chairman of the Bowling Green Association, "when in fact their story is more glorious, more inspiring, more difficult to comprehend than the Pilgrims of Plymouth Rock and their good fortune eight years later."

But history, Piccolo laments, may not be written by the winners as much as by those who know how to tell a good story.

Speaking of which, did you hear the one about Roy Block, a direct descendant of the Dutch explorer? He worked for years as a marine surveyor for the government at 45 Broadway, the very site of Adriaen Block's little settlement. Roy Block died in 1967. His survivors included a son, John, who lived in Queens until about a decade ago.

Are any descendants of Adriaen Block still out there? Does any know how to tell a good story?

November 27, 2008

Don't Settle for Less

Four hundred years ago next month, King James II empowered the Virginia Council of London to establish a British settlement in North America. Its stockholders were hungry for gold, committed to converting savages, and seeking a shortcut to the Orient.

They sent three ships with 144 sailors and settlers who founded a colony on a marshy peninsula jutting into the James River.

Now, the place is billing itself as the nation's birthplace, the first permanent English colony, the site of America's 400th anniversary. On May 14, 1607, according to an official account, the colonists came ashore—never to leave.

Except for one thing. They left.

By the end of the seventeenth century, after creating a legacy that included slavery and profiteering from tobacco, the Jamestown settlement had all but vanished. And today, with all due respect to Virginia and to its very able historians and tourist bureau, as Gertrude Stein once said of her native Oakland, in Jamestown there is no there, there—not very much there, anyway.

Jamestown's permanent population right now? Two people—an archaeologist and his wife.

If any place deserves to be known as the nation's birthplace, it's New York, population 8.2 million. And a real birthday is almost here.

Perhaps it has slipped your mind, but 2009 is the 400th anniversary of Henry Hudson's voyage up what became his eponymous river. It's also 400 years since Samuel de Champlain sailed down his lake upstate. I guess to keep us from becoming too giddy too soon, the 200th anniversary of Robert Fulton's inaugural steamboat voyage up the Hudson in 1807 is being marked in 2009, also.

One hundred years ago, the Hudson tricentenary was a big deal. It lasted two weeks. Wilbur Wright flew from Governors Island to Grant's Tomb and back.

Hundreds of vessels paraded up the river, including a replica of Hudson's *Half Moon*, which unfortunately sailed smack into the facsimile of Fulton's *Clermont*.

Here's some film news trivia, by the way: In *The New World*, the recent Terence Malik film about Jamestown, the role of the colonists' lead ship was played by a replica of the *Half Moon*, which normally plies the Hudson.

In 1909, Americans looked back 300 years, to when the *Half Moon*'s mate wrote that the first New Yorkers weren't all that different from today—at least on one count: "They desire clothes," the journal said, "and are very civil."

The chief controversy then, at least in the pages of the *Times*, was whether Hudson, who was English and happened to be a friend of Captain John Smith of Jamestown fame, should be referred to as Hendrik or Henry.

This time, around, there's no such controversy—by the way, it's Henry—at least not yet, because few New Yorkers even know about the celebration. There might be some confusion, again, though, over a name, since the initials of the Hudson Fulton Champlain evoke not so much our rich heritage and diversity as they do the Household Finance Corporation.

Ken Jackson, the Columbia University history professor and editor of *The Encyclopedia of New York City*, doesn't begrudge Jamestown its eighteen-month-long quadricentennial—it's not that Jamestown isn't important, he says. But that the contrast with New York couldn't be greater."

America, he says, begins in New York.

May 25, 2006

9/11

I used to measure life in four-year increments—the time it took, after uprooting myself from Brooklyn and transplanting myself upstate, to graduate from college.

At some point, that template got tired. Not that life becomes less compartmentalized. We still contrive more or less arbitrary time frames, except they tend to be imposed by others: Summer abruptly ends on a September Monday originally designated to honor working people, but which, in New York, has become synonymous with celebrating West Indian heritage. Meanwhile, organized labor, unwilling to interrupt its long weekend for an obligatory march, stages its own parade five years later.

Or anniversaries. What makes the fifth somehow more significant than, say, the fourth?

This year, 2006, is, of course, the fifth anniversary of 9/11. Since that horrific morning, lots of people have come and gone. Incredibly, maybe one in ten of today's New Yorkers was not even living here then.

Most of us who were here went on with our lives. We're reassured somewhat by the visible police presence, coupled with declining crime. We still empathize with cops, firefighters, and other first responders, though we're only belatedly coming to grips with their physical symptoms. We've gotten more used to removing our shoes at airports without complaining. Instead of looking the other way, we're a little more likely to say something if we see something suspicious.

It's nothing short of miraculous that we haven't been attacked again. And, presumably, inevitable that someday we might be. Then what? New

Yorkers, as usual, proved themselves resilient the last time. But as one police official told me, this is not Tel Aviv. We have not yet been hardened—let's hope we never have to be—to the prospect of random suicide bombers or worse committed to creating perpetual havoc and sabotaging the city's economy.

Five years later, though, most of us are still largely looking back.

Not long after 9/11, I looked back even further. I visited Pearl Harbor. The parallels with Ground Zero were striking. Both sites bore witness to disaster, not victory. Both were the result of sneak attacks that punctured the myth of American invincibility.

Professor Edward Linenthal of the University of Wisconsin calls the U.S.S. *Arizona*, which was built at the Brooklyn Navy Yard, a unique relic. It's in an active navy base where, quite literally, the world changed. It's a historic site without any of the physical boundaries that demarcate sacred space at other battlefields. It took two decades to build a memorial. And what produced my most poignant memory of Pearl Harbor was something the monument's designers never anticipated: Every day, about a quart of oil bubbles up from somewhere inside the barely submerged battleship. The U.S.S. *Arizona* still weeps black tears.

At Ground Zero, a new tribute center has just opened across the street. And with better teamwork from a new governor, the pace of development, including an appropriate memorial, is likely to accelerate. In five more years, downtown will be very different.

Meanwhile, the images of 9/11 are seared in our mind's eye. One newly published collection of before-and-after photographs was taken by Joel Meyerowitz, who had unusual access to the site. He provides, as he puts it, "a window for everyone else who wanted to be there, too—to help, or to grieve, or simply to try to understand what had happened to our city."

Another book, *The Stories Behind the Images of 9/11*, includes a snapshot by a Port Authority employee, John Labriola. It's of a young fireman climbing the stairs in the north tower. In the end, Garrison Keillor wrote the other day in a *Times* book review, "the images become common and one turns to words to find the reality."

These words are John Labriola's. He said, "The one conclusion I came to on 9/11 is that people in the stairwell were in a state of grace. They helped each other. They didn't panic. Most people are basically good. I knew this, with certainty, because I had gone through the crucible. What a great example people left: be selfless, help the person around you, and get through it."

Looking back or ahead, as another four years go by, or even five, and we take the measure of time passing, that's one example we ought not forget.

September 7, 2006

The World Trade Center Memorial, a landscaped plaza with the names of 9/11 victims displayed around two square voids where the towers stood, opened in time for the tenth anniversary of the attacks. The National September 11 Memorial and Museum was formally dedicated in 2014.

Dutch Treats

What do bowling, the Bowery, Brooklyn, the Bronx, Harlem, Stuyvesant Town, the Yankees, the Roosevelts, and coleslaw have in common?

They're all part of New York's unique Dutch heritage. You might have missed it, with the economic crisis and the UN General Assembly traffic jams, but Dutch officials, including the prime minister, the foreign minister, and the heir to the Dutch throne, were also in town to inaugurate the city's 400th birthday celebration.

The party begins unofficially in 2009, with the quadricentennial of Henry Hudson's voyage up what became the eponymous river. It's also 400 years since Samuel de Champlain sailed down his lake upstate and the official bicentennial of Robert Fulton's inaugural steamboat voyage.

Given the debate that's been provoked over in which year New York was actually founded, the Hudson celebration is likely to revive competing claims over which Eastern Hemisphere explorer came first.

Verrazzano, an Italian sailing for the French, anchored off Brooklyn in 1524 and described a large lake that was probably the Upper Bay. The Spanish dispatched Esteban Gomez, a black navigator from Portugal. He arrived on St. Anthony's Day in 1526 and christened the river the San Antonio.

Since neither explorer discovered much of great value, Europeans apparently decided New York wasn't a nice place to live, *or* to visit. Hudson— an Englishman presciently hired by the Dutch—didn't make it here until more than eighty years later, in 1609. The crew was a bit wary, but his first mate described the first New Yorkers he encountered as "very civil." Perhaps as a harbinger of our becoming a fashion capital, he observed, "They desire clothes."

In September 1909, the 300th anniversary of Hudson's arrival was a very big deal. Wilbur Wright took off from Governors Island and flew up the Hudson to Grant's Tomb and back. A flotilla of hundreds of vessels included a replica of Hudson's *Half Moon*, which, lamentably, sailed smack into a facsimile of Robert Fulton's *Clermont*.

Celebrants were cautioned about attracting pickpockets by appearing "too prosperous." They were told that cops had orders to arrest "elbowers." And in a warning that resonates today, they were urged, to say something "if you see anyone acting in a suspicious manner."

New York is still home to about 25,000 people who claim Dutch ancestry, but that's fewer than most other ethnic groups. Much of the Dutch legacy seems tied to ING's sponsorship of the New York City Marathon and to the talk about reviving windmills.

Recently, visiting Dutch officials planted a hickory sapling on Governors Island (which the Dutch first named after the nut trees that grew there). They plan to open a Dutch pavilion in Rockefeller Center, and later move it to tiny Peter Minuit Plaza, at the Battery. They hope to install street signs downtown with the original Dutch names.

They also intend to exhibit here for the first time Peter Schaghen's 1626 letter announcing to the "High and Mighty Lords" of the West India Company that the settlers in Lower Manhattan were in good spirits; had borne some children; grew wheat, barley, and other grain; and bought the roughly 22,000-acre island for 60 guilders' worth of goods.

Today the Netherlands is grappling with an issue that New Yorkers came to grips with 400 years ago. It's called diversity. Yes, there were slaves in early New Amsterdam. There was some anti-Semitism. But Peter Stuyvesant resisted orders from the high and mighty lords back home in Holland to get rid of, among others, the Swedes.

"What we now call tolerance was really indifference, as long as you behaved," Frans Timmermans, the Dutch minister for international affairs, told me.

The influx of Moroccans and Turks is changing the face of the Netherlands. In major cities, almost half the population is no longer of European origin.

"We still call people immigrants or foreigners in the third generation,"

Timmermans said. "You've never had an integration policy by the government, and yet this is the most successful immigrant society. The day you step off the boat or plane you're a New Yorker. That has to do with its history. People who know where they come from know where they want to go."

September 25, 2008

Washington Squared

A century ago, Henry James returned to New York after living abroad for two decades. He was appalled at how the Lower Manhattan neighborhood of his youth had been transformed into a place he pronounced an impermanent, alien, shrill, blighted, and "vast crude democracy of trade."

Summing up before tackling Newport in his survey of the American scene, James sounded exhilarated and exhausted, as he well might today. All he could exclaim was, "Remarkable, unspeakable New York!"

He especially hated the skyscrapers.

"Crowned not only with no history, but with no credible possibility of time for history," he wrote, "and consecrated by no uses save the commercial at any cost, they are simply the most piercing notes in that concert of the expensively provisional into which your supreme sense of New York resolves itself."

His birthplace on Washington Place had already been demolished to accommodate a ten-story building, which he described as "a high, square, impersonal structure, proclaiming its lack of interest with a crudity all its own."

"The effect for me, in Washington Place, was of having been amputated of half my history," James wrote.

Less than a decade later, 146 employees of the Triangle Shirtwaist company would die there in a horrific fire. Today, James would find the loft building still there. It's now a New York University science building.

The 1830s Greek Revival houses on Washington Square North, where his grandmother lived, would look largely familiar, except for the garage entrance in a five-story red-brick apartment house. The door to Number 18 is flanked by tasteful plaques, but they don't mention the site's history as the setting of James's novel *Washington Square*. Instead, they advertise the offices of a urologist and a cosmetic surgeon.

In his novel, he wrote, "round the corner was the more august precinct of the Fifth Avenue, taking its origin at this point with a spacious and confident air which already marked it for high destinies."

Higher than he could have imagined. Sauntering up Fifth Avenue, past MacDougal Alley and Washington Mews, which largely retain their nineteenth-century charm, James would pass a twenty-one-story apartment building, about as high as the tallest skyscraper in 1906.

Somewhere around 8th Street, he recorded a Proustian moment—the smells of a bakery that he called "a blessed repository of doughnuts, cookies, creamcakes and pies." Today the smell of baked goods still emanates from Le Pain Quotidien, a waffle shop, and a place that specializes in cream puffs. Hot dog smells waft from a Gray's Papaya.

At 10th Street, he could still pause to reflect on the Church of the Ascension, an English Gothic edifice built in 1840. Or, if he had taken Sixth Avenue instead, he would have recognized Bigelow drugstore, the pyramidal turret of the old Jefferson Market Courthouse, now a library, and, farther up the avenue, the restored department stores on the elegant Ladies' Mile.

On West 14th Street, he would have found his house long demolished, replaced first by Jacob Rothschild's millinery store (it had branches in Brooklyn and Paris) and, early in the twentieth century, by an unattractive five-story building, soon to be topped by several more floors of apartments. The site is flanked by a Starbucks—James might have appreciated the allusion to the first mate in *Moby-Dick*—and a storefront that sells electronics gear and luggage.

James's impressions of *New York Revisited* were recorded in *Harper's Magazine* and excerpted in the *New York Times*.

If he revisited a century later, what would James say?

"I think that the Master would have the power of thought to be delighted by the ongoing exuberance of Lower Manhattan," said Professor Harold Bloom, the literary scholar at Yale.

"I think James's imagination would be stimulated by the subway, given his sensitivity to the surreal and the subterranean in our consciousness," said Lyndall Gordon, a James biographer.

Professor John Auchard of the University of Maryland, who has also written about James, recalled the novelist's exuberant response to immigrant ghettoes and to the Bowery.

"I think, above all, the high-culture Mandarin Henry James would have regretted the transformation of the Lower East Side, and other parts of the city, into something that begins to approximate a mall," Professor Auchard said. "Today James might wish to chomp on a pastrami sandwich in a remote corner of Katz's Deli on East Houston, but he might do so with unspeakable Jamesian dread of the Starbucks inching up the block." (Katz's opened in 1888, but there is no evidence that James ate pastrami there.)

June 1, 2006

Turnstile Justice

At precisely 1:23 P.M. on June 14, a Lexington Avenue local is supposed to head downtown from the Pelham Bay Park station in the Bronx. Trains don't usually leave the station at that time, but this one is scheduled to depart on a special subway timetable to accommodate passengers going to and from the Puerto Rican Day parade.

What makes the time especially tantalizing is that two days earlier, the latest version of *The Taking of Pelham 123* was to have opened in movie theaters. The film is a promising remake of a movie about four subterranean pirates who hijack a subway train—designated as Pelham 123 for the time it left its Bronx starting point that afternoon.

Watching the original, you'd no longer recognize either New York (the fare was thirty-five cents) or its post-macho mayor.

The film was based on a book written in the final days of the Lindsay administration. The Brooklyn-born author died a few years ago, so it's uncertain who inspired him. But the movie's make-believe mayor seemed to combine the persona of Abe Beame, who won the Democratic nomination that year, with just a hint of the feisty Ed Koch, who withdrew from the 1973 race but would defeat Beame four years later.

"The mayor was ineffectual, a ditz, a *kvetch*," Lee Wallace, the Brooklyn-born actor who portrayed the mayor (and did so again in *Batman*), recalled the other day. "He was overwhelmed and manipulated by his wife and his deputy."

A *Times* movie reviewer concurred, writing that Wallace "makes a pleasing, indecisive slob of a mayor—aware that he'll be booed by any random crowd."

New York's celluloid mayors have generally performed even worse than the real ones, with the possible exception of Al Pacino in *City Hall*. Think Purnell Pratt in the Marx Brothers's *A Night at the Opera* or David Margulies playing Lenny the mayor in *Ghostbusters* or the cartoonish Rod Steiger in *January Man*.

New York itself wasn't performing much better in 1974. The city was much grittier then, although the Lindsay administration, hoping to put on the best face, insisted that the filmmakers use a graffiti-free subway car.

"New York is a mess," *Times* film critic Vincent Canby conceded back then. "It's also getting worse all the time."

Nonetheless, Canby pronounced *Pelham 123* "a good-humored, often witty suspense melodrama in which the representatives of law and decency triumph without bending the rules." He added, though: "If you have to take any form of public transportation to and from the theater where it's playing, you may find its conclusions wildly improbable."

Thirty-five years later, the mayor and the people who run the subway system have considerably less to apologize for. They didn't have to search for a graffiti-free train (although subway buffs, who ridiculed a television version filmed in Toronto and released in 1998, will again likely leap on a number of technical improbabilities).

This time, the city's film office took a precaution that might have seemed pointless in the 1970s when "shooting" evoked mayhem, not movies: The filmmakers were requested to limit their make-believe gunfire so as not to alarm nearby residents.

And this time the mayor of New York is being played by James Gandolfini of *Sopranos* fame.

"I would think it would be quite different," Wallace said. "I don't know that he would play that kind of buffoon."

In fact, Gandolfini plays a Wall Street guy—echoes of Michael Bloomberg. He's described as more in command than his 1974 predecessor, but still a victim of his own impatience and overconfidence, which lead to tactical miscalculations. ("I left my Rudy Giuliani suit at home," "Mayor" Gandolfini says in the film.)

In the original film, the hijackers demand $1 million in ransom to free the eighteen passengers trapped underground in a single subway car. The sniveling mayor meets with his wife, Jessie, played by Doris Roberts, and his deputy, Warren LaSalle, played by Tony Roberts. He ponders how the public will react.

> *Mayor:* What are they going to say, Warren?
> *Deputy Mayor Warren LaSalle:* "They" who?
> *Mayor:* Who? Everybody—the press, the man on the street.
> *Mayor's wife, Jessie:* He means the voters.
> *Deputy Mayor:* You know what they're going to say. The *Times* is going to support you. The *News* is going to knock you. The *Post* will take both sides at the same time. The rich will support you. . . . So come on, Al, quit stalling!
> *Mayor:* Will you stop bullying everybody, Warren? This is supposed to be a democracy!
> *Deputy Mayor:* Wise up, for chrissake, we're trying to run a city, not a goddamn democracy! . . . We've got to pay!
> *Mayor:* Jessie, Jessie, what do you say?
> *Mayor's wife:* I know a million dollars sounds like a lot of money. But just think what you'll get in return.
> *Mayor:* What?
> *Mayor's wife:* Eighteen sure votes.
> *Mayor:* All right, all right. Warren, Warren, arrange for the payoff!

A million dollars for eighteen votes! That's even more than Mayor Bloomberg spent.

April 16, 2009

The Green Book

There are two version of how Vincent Impellitteri, an obscure law secretary to an obscure judge, was chosen for the Democratic mayoral ticket in 1945.

The darker version is that Impellitteri was foisted on Bill O'Dwyer, the favorite for mayor, by East Harlem congressman Vito Marcantonio, and that Marcantonio was fronting for a budding mobster named Tommy Lucchese.

The more benign version is that party leaders simply plucked his name from the index of the official city directory. O'Dwyer was Irish, from Brooklyn. Lazarus Joseph, the candidate for comptroller, was Jewish and from the Bronx. To balance the ticket, Tammany Democrats needed a Manhattan Italian for City Council president.

"We flipped through *The Green Book*," said Bert Stand, the secretary of Tammany Hall, "for the longest Italian name we could find."

Either way, Impellitteri was elected Council president. He would later succeed O'Dwyer as mayor of New York. Temporarily stumped, tabloid headline writers shortened the name to Impy, but Impellitteri remains the longest surname in the history of New York's mayors.

The 2008 edition of *The Green Book*—the official directory of the City of New York—has just been published. The cover is green again, as it has been for all but one of the previous seventy-nine editions—the last one, in 2005, when the book was wrapped in orange. That was in homage to the more or less saffron-colored fabric of the *Gates* art installation that graced Central Park earlier that year, thanks to the artists Christo and Jeanne-Claude.

The directory was first published in 1918, at 112 pages. The origins of the green cover, like the legends surrounding Mayor Impellitteri, are ambiguous.

The latest version is an unabashed advertisement for the environment. The front cover is dominated by a stylized Statue of Liberty. Her torch is a compact fluorescent lamp. The back cover, where the mayor's name also appears, proclaims, "Help Make NYC Greener."

Originally dubbed *The Little Green Book*, it's green, again, but not little. Since 2005 alone, it has grown by another 14 pages—to 660, before the index of names (although, in fairness, the directory also lists county, state, federal, and even United Nations officials).

Even with the advent of the Internet, *The Green Book* is to the desks of City Hall Kremlinologists what, as Dick Shepard once wrote in the *Times*, Gideon's Bible is to a hotel escritoire. In 1926, the *Times* reported two mysterious changes: Mayor Jimmy Walker's name was conspicuously missing from the cover, and a previous account of his administration's "alleged achievements" was also deleted.

In the 1970s, Robert Moses's name was dropped—he was still a consultant to the Triborough Bridge and Tunnel Authority. The omission, Shepard wrote, was akin to dropping Scarlett O'Hara from *Gone with the Wind*. Another year, the title page was torn out of thousands of copies because the comptroller's middle initial was wrong.

During the Depression, the directory was condensed to only thirty-two pages, reflecting the city's fiscal condition more than the shrinking of the executive payroll. During World War II, publication was suspended to save paper. It was again, under Mayor Lindsay, in the early 1970s, but was resumed in 1974, under Abe Beame.

"I suspect," Fred Ferretti wrote in a *Times* book review, "that either Mayor Beame was becoming irked at having people continually call 566-5700 and ask why John Lindsay wasn't plowing the side streets out in Bellerose, or he simply wanted a *Green Book* with *his* name in gold on the cover, too."

In 1976, a special bicentennial edition celebrated the titles of some of New York's earliest officials, now generally, but not universally, considered to be anachronistic. They included the Public Whipper and the City Scavenger.

In 1985, bowing to popular usage, the official name of the official directory was changed to *The Green Book*.

The book, on sale for $19.95, with ten pages of updates already, also includes a helpful guide to where to apply for licenses, including a permit to shorten your employees' lunch hour to less than thirty minutes. If you're thinking of opening an appearance-enhancement shop, you're referred to the listing for beauty parlors—but there isn't one. There's an entry for "captives," but they are within the jurisdiction of the state Insurance Department, not law enforcement.

I've always been most fascinated by the index of names, as an unscientific gauge of the demography of government. Mayor Bloomberg has six entries, the same as Vincent E. Green, who is a deputy investigation commissioner and inspector general in several agencies. Bill Thompson, the comptroller, is listed eight times. Martha Stark, the finance commissioner, is most ubiquitous, with eleven listings.

Mayor Impellitteri, who succeeded the last certifiably Irish mayor, was himself followed by Robert F. Wagner, who was half Irish. When Wagner was mayor, the appropriately named *Green Book* included fifty-three municipal officials whose names began with O'. By 1990, there were half as many. The latest *Green Book* lists fourteen—outnumbered, this time, by the sixteen Rodriguezes.

September 6, 2007

Thanks for the Lift

When I was a kid, my favorite book was *The Taxi That Hurried*. To occupy me while my sister took piano lessons, my grandmother would read it aloud. Again and again. But, the fact is, growing up in Brownsville, Brooklyn, I can't remember ever taking a taxi. *The Taxi That Hurried*—that 1946 book about a conscientious New York cabbie rushing a little boy and his mom through horrendous traffic to catch a train at Grand Central and honking all the way—took place in The City, in Manhattan. The locale seemed perfectly natural.

Contrast my experience with that of my youngest son, Will. He was born and grew up in Manhattan. His first word, literally? *Taxi*—with his tiny toddler arm extended at the requisite angle.

What evokes my personal taxi memories isn't the latest dispute over whether cabs should be equipped with tracking devices. Rather, we're on the brink of another unheralded anniversary in New York: the introduction of the first metered, motorized taxis exactly one hundred years ago.

The use of metering to measure distance traveled by a vehicle for hire was nothing new. It's been traced to first-century Rome, to a device that dropped a stone into a receptacle underneath a carriage at every 1,000 paces. At the end of the ride, the driver computed the fare by counting the stones.

As Graham Russell Gao Hodges explains in his new social history, titled *Taxi*, modern cab driving stems from a grudge.

Harry N. Allen, a New Yorker who graduated from NYU when he

was only seventeen, was angry because the driver of a horse-drawn hansom cab had charged him $5 for the ride from 44th Street to 57th Street.

So, a few months later, on October 1, 1907, Allen inaugurated motor cab service—sixty-five distinctive bright red gasoline-powered cars punctuated with green trim—from six Manhattan hotels. He promised hundreds more. His drivers, wearing blue-gray-and-black braided uniforms, resembled West Point cadets.

Allen, an import–export executive who became a stockbroker, was even credited with coining the term *taxicab*. He explained that *taxi* was derived from the French-made *taximetres*, which registered the tax, or fare, for horse-drawn cabs.

The fare in his taxis was structured pretty much the way it is today: 30 cents for the first half-mile, 10 cents for each additional quarter-mile, and 10 cents for each six minutes of waiting time. But, adjusting for inflation, the trip was probably more expensive than it is today. A two-mile ride, or about forty blocks, originally cost 90 cents, which in those days was close to $20.

When Allen introduced his taxis, the city already had nearly 4,000 cabs—most of them horse-drawn and unmetered. Like any transition in New York, this one was typically tumultuous. Rivalry erupted between drivers of unmetered horse-drawn cabs and of Allen's motorized, metered service. It played out in lawsuits and street violence.

Even tipping was controversial.

Allen insisted that Americans are "always apt to express their satisfaction at good treatment."

But several *Times* readers complained, including one who signed his letter "Taxpayer." He, or she, wrote, "The tip is essentially an expression of gratitude and generosity from a superior to a supposedly poorly paid inferior. Now, in America the masses recognize no superiors, and the worker exacts a fitting wage through unions and certain scarcities of labor.... Thus, with the absence of superiors, and assured adequate wages, the necessity for tipping ends: tipping becomes un-American."

By the end of one year, Allen had 700 cabs operating. The horse was doomed. Harmony in the hack industry was short-lived, though. Drivers went on strike. One scab was beaten to death. A young bystander was shot by strikebreakers.

Allen won his battle but lost the war. He went out of business within a few years. Taxis endured. So did tips. Uniforms didn't, but the drivers did, as a unique breed evolving over time. Hacking, Graham Hodges writes in *Taxi*, "took on a mythic quality as an entry-level trade by which an immigrant could work toward the success of the next generation."

A hundred years later, it still is.

June 19, 2008

While the number of taxi medallions was frozen, cabbies suddenly found themselves vulnerable to competition from car services like Lyft and Uber, which flooded Midtown with their vehicles.

The Latest Poop

Ed Koch told me not long ago that he was lonely. He said he was even thinking of taking Harry Truman's advice about the cut-throat political culture in the nation's capital—advice that, arguably, is just as relevant to New York.

In Washington, Truman once said, if you want a friend, get a dog.

Koch, the former mayor, says he won't get one, though. Not because he's worried about the competition, that passersby might pay more attention to the dog than to him. He says he just can't bear the thought of picking up after his pet.

New York's so-called canine waste law was passed 30 years ago to deal with the estimated 20,000 tons of poop deposited annually on city streets. And what's so poignant about Koch's pet peeve is that the law took effect in 1978, the first year he was mayor.

Like a few other statutes—the automobile seat belt law, for one—it coupled common sense with peer pressure and penalties for noncompliance to make a tangible difference in public behavior, and in record time.

Koch vowed to vigorously enforce the law. And it worked.

What brought this to mind, in addition to being reminded every day when I pick up after my own dog, was the horse that died after getting spooked by a drummer on Central Park South.

We still have horses in New York City. Hundreds of them.

You don't have to conjure them up by going to see *Spamalot* and hear the clip-clopping of coconuts being banged together. We've still got the real thing. Their sounds, and smells, evoke the New York of Henry James

171

and Edith Wharton—although, I admit, that's probably a lot better for the romantics among us than it is for the horses themselves.

We rightly complain today about pollution and horn honking by cars and trucks. But—and sorry if you're hearing or reading this at breakfast—imagine what New York was like when 100,000 or so horses plied the streets and nobody picked up after them. I mean, if Ed Koch is skittish about picking up after a little dog . . . .

That's how many horses the Department of Health's Sanitary Bureau counted a century ago. The same census found about 8,000 stables in the city.

A new book, *The Horse in the City*, recalls a *Times* editorial from 1881 which complained that horse droppings "make street-filth especially disgusting." Invoking a verb that has largely vanished as an urban anachronism, the editorial described many thoroughfares as "incessantly manured."

In 1907, when motorized coaches first began carrying passengers on Fifth Avenue, the remaining horse-drawn streetcars traveled at about twenty miles per hour. That's faster than most vehicles move in Midtown today.

As recently as eighty years ago, horse auctions were still regularly held on East 24th Street, although the sturdy French and Belgian stallions imported before World War I or bred in the Midwest were becoming harder to find. The best could haul a 5,000-pound wagon. They were probably cheaper to feed than cars at gas prices these days. And they would work from seven to ten years, on average, which is longer than most vehicles last reliably today.

But except for the stalwarts who delivered milk and hauled itinerant peddlers and junkmen, horses were rapidly displaced by cars and trucks. The city fathers even predicted that New York would follow the example of—appropriately enough—Detroit, and ban horses altogether.

Today, the Health Department doesn't keep count of privately owned horses for recreational riding or of police horses—either the equine or the wooden ones. The city counts only licensed carriage horses, like the ones on Central Park South. At last count, there were 297.

"Let him be considered indispensable, as an instrument," the nineteenth-century *Times* editorial thundered, "until some better instrument enables us to dispense with him."

Horses survived the advent of steam, electricity, bicycles, and, to a lesser extent, the automobile.

As the essayist E. S. Nadal noted in the *Times* a few years after the editorial, "It will still be difficult for the smartest automobile to compete with a smart cab drawn by a smart horse."

Cars still produce polluting exhaust fumes. But necessity being the mother of invention—a necessity born, in part, of popular embrace of the pooper-scooper law—many New York carriage horses today come fully equipped with diapers.

September 27, 2007

Let Them Eat Their Words

What did Gerald Ford and Marie Antoinette have in com-mon?

I could think of only one thing: Being misquoted cost both of them their jobs.

In Hollywood's latest Marie Antoinette biopic, the French queen de-nies what may well have been a half-baked story that she callously urged breadless peasants to eat cake instead. "I never said that," the actress Kirsten Dunst pouts. "I wonder why people keep saying I did."

Ford, on October 29, 1975, gave a speech denying federal assistance to spare New York from bankruptcy. The front-page headline of the next day's *Daily News* read: "Ford to City: Drop Dead."

I was city editor of the *News* back then. I remember my bosses, Mike O'Neill and Bill Brink, returning from lunch that day and asking for the gist of Ford's speech. Their consensus: that he had told the city, "Screw you," or words to that effect. Brink couched it as succinctly, but more discreetly: "Drop dead."

Yes, the truth is, Ford never explicitly said, "Drop dead." Yet those two words were, arguably, the essence of his speech. As he later acknowledged, they probably cost him the presidency the following year when he nar-rowly lost New York.

Ford would always insist that the headline was inaccurate and unfair.

Yet two weeks before the Drop Dead speech, on a day Ford had also rebuffed New York's appeals to raise cash, the city was so close to the brink that a press release was drafted and typed announcing that the city was bankrupt.

The statement by Mayor Abe Beame, which a former mayoral adviser found the other day, said: "I have been advised by the comptroller that the City of New York has insufficient cash on hand to meet debt obligations due today. This constitutes the default that we have struggled to avoid."

Beame's statement was never released, but only because Albert Shanker of the teachers' union finally furnished $150 million from the union's pension fund. (Remember that question from Woody Allen's film *Sleeper*? What triggered a world-wide atomic war? The answer: "A man named Albert Shanker got hold of a nuclear warhead.")

But Ford's view that he actually helped New York is echoed in evolving historical revisionism. Some would argue that his public recalcitrance bought time for the city to make its case to an even more reluctant Congress. Also, that he forced the city to put its fiscal house in order.

And less than two months after saying or meaning or merely implying "Drop dead"—or resorting to tough love by holding the city's feet to the fire—Ford signed legislation to provide federal loans to the city.

Gerald Ford left another legacy to New York.

Without even trying, Ford had more or less stumbled into the presidency in 1974 in the wake of the Watergate scandal. But the man who became his vice president through the same historical quirk—Nelson Rockefeller—not only always wanted the top job but defined his professional life by it.

Not long after Ford enlisted him, I asked Rockefeller whether he had accepted the vice presidency as his last, best vehicle to the White House. After persistent questioning, he blurted out his answer with the exasperation of a harried commuter racing to catch the last train.

"What," he replied, "do you think I'm doing here?"

Rockefeller was confirmed by Congress, but only after he confronted what he said was the "myth" about his wealth (by today's standards, he would barely qualify as a billionaire). "Would my family background somehow limit and blind me, so that I would not be able to see and serve the general good of all Americans?" he asked, then replied helpfully: "Poverty, too, can blind a man or a woman. Some never rise above the hungry resentments of early hardships."

But within less than a year, Rockefeller was sacrificed to the party's conservative wing. He was jettisoned as Ford's expected running mate.

Ford won the nomination, but it didn't matter. He was defeated by

Jimmy Carter, whom the Democrats had—not coincidentally—nominated in New York.

On January 19, 1977, Rockefeller's last night as vice president, he finally got to the White House, however briefly. He, his wife, and their children were invited by Gerald Ford to sleep over.

December 28, 2006

Four-Star Finale

Now that the latest anniversary of 9/11 is behind us, with Wall Street rescued by Washington and New Yorkers sleeping easier because Mayor Bloomberg has decided to run again, it's okay to read *The City's End*.

Otherwise, you might find it just a bit too creepy to wade into a book that, as its subtitle suggests, encompasses "Two Centuries of Fantasies, Fears and Premonitions of New York's Destruction."

The book by Max Page, an architecture and history professor at the University of Massachusetts in Amherst, doesn't celebrate the mostly mythical apocalypses. Rather, it explores why this city's end has been invoked repeatedly as a cultural device—by perpetrators ranging from W. E. B. Du Bois to Upton Sinclair, from Orson Welles to Will Smith.

From the earliest urban legends to the latest computer games, Page argues, Americans embraced fantasies of the city's destruction as "a reaffirmation of New York's greatness."

"We destroy New York on film and paper," he writes, "by telling stories of clear and present dangers, with causes and effects, villains and heroes, to make our world more comprehensible than it has become."

Upheaval seems to have been taken for granted.

In 1907, the *New York Times* published a brief article about Horace Johnson, a Connecticut farmer who had correctly predicted the Great Blizzard of 1888 and the San Francisco earthquake. This time, he was forecasting an imminent massive quake that would sink Manhattan. The dispassionate headline read simply, "Will Destroy New York."

Page reminds us, though, that much of our mythical mayhem has been self-inflicted—with the vehicle lately being environmental disasters unleashed by an aggrieved Mother Nature.

The book jacket portrays the darker side of human nature: that menacing 1950 *Collier's* magazine cover that envisioned an atomic blast over Manhattan—an image that probably hastened the exodus to the suburbs.

New Yorkers suddenly felt vulnerable to foreign and domestic terrorists. In Woody Allen's futuristic film *Sleeper*, a character blames the end of civilization as we know it on the volatile leader of the city's teachers' union—all because "a man named Albert Shanker got hold of a nuclear warhead."

What makes New York a magnet for mayhem, real and imagined? Page invokes that charming *New Yorker* cartoon of King Kong and Godzilla nonchalantly strolling past havoc as Manhattanites flee before them. "Let's face it," the scaly monster says cheerfully to his furry friend, "the city's in our blood."

And in a remake of *The Day the Earth Stood Still*, the moment of truth occurs, of course, in New York . . . where nothing ever stands still for long.

As far back as 1824, hundreds of gullible New Yorkers were hoodwinked into believing that overdevelopment would tip Lower Manhattan into the bay. By the early twentieth century, change was such a constant that Henry James was pronouncing New York "a provisional city." About the same time, O. Henry said famously that "it'll be a great place if they ever finish it."

Funny, but we took one belated step toward finishing it just the other day. Twenty-nine months since ground was broken—more than twice as long as it took to finish the Empire State Building—a brand-new discount Broadway tickets booth, topped by seating on a shimmering glass staircase, opened in Times Square.

You might have gotten an advance glimpse of it last year in the film *I Am Legend*. Will Smith, the lone survivor of a viral epidemic, walks through the square, which is deserted except for a mountain lion perched atop the TKTS booth.

But the fiberglass booth and the staircase took so long to install that the filmmakers couldn't wait. They built a replica in the Bronx. "It's the first time," said Nick Leahy, the project's architect, that "I've seen a building destroyed before it was completed."

You can't really stand still for long in Times Square, but now you can sit. A surprise ending, even by New York standards.

October 16, 2008

Home, Sweet Home

Teddy Roosevelt once broke in, smashing a window, when he returned to find the house locked and the help asleep.

Al Smith kept a menagerie in the back yard—including a 350-pound black bear that wandered off and made itself at home next door, to the delight of the orphans who lived there. Four monkeys also once bolted, only to return on their own the next morning, after what must have been a disappointing night on the town in Albany.

Nelson Rockefeller escaped a smoky fire out a second-floor window during a rare sleepover.

Mario Cuomo almost never left.

George Pataki hardly ever stayed.

Governor-elect Eliot Spitzer bought a house in nearby Columbia County, and two of his teenage daughters will finish high school in New York City and live with their mother in the Spitzers' Manhattan apartment. As for living in Albany, Spitzer says he'll spend "as much time there as necessary to do the job."

Welcome to New York's official governor's residence, to the gloomy-looking 40-odd-room Charles Addams–esque patchwork of Victorian turrets, cupolas, bays, and gingerbread. It celebrates its 150th birthday next year.

Things could be worse. The house could be called Drumthwacket, that Scottish and Gaelic tongue twister, which loosely translates as "wooded hill." It's the official residence of the governor of New Jersey—in Princeton, a leafy refuge fifteen miles from the capital, Trenton.

New York's governor's residence, on Eagle Street, is a convenient stone's throw from the Capitol—actually, a Bible was once hurled onto the grounds while Cuomo was governor.

For all its "variety," as a guidebook sanguinely puts it, and the fact that it stands on a bluff once known as "Gallows Hill," the Albany residence goes by a most prosaic name: the Executive Mansion.

The house on Eagle Street was built by an Albany banker. Governor Samuel J. Tilden rented it in 1875. His successor persuaded the state to buy it.

The mansion has three full floors, but many more stories.

One guidebook claims it has housed more presidents of the United States (including Grover Cleveland and both Roosevelts) than any other American residence except the White House.

Governor Cornell blamed the plumbing for an outbreak of malaria.

Governor Flower limited his workday to five hours, including his lunch hour at the mansion.

Governor Black and his family lived there only during the legislative session, because he couldn't afford the upkeep.

Governor Hill, a bachelor, complained that the place was too cramped, and nearly doubled its size.

His successor, Governor Morton, arrived with ten servants and also found it too small.

Franklin Roosevelt, afflicted with polio, installed an elevator and a swimming pool.

During the Depression, Governor Lehman skimped on maintenance until a ceiling collapsed during the annual dinner for the Court of Appeals—worse, still, his brother was the chief judge.

Guests have included Albert Einstein and Winston Churchill and Presidents Grant, Taft, and Eisenhower. When Princess Beatrix of the Netherlands visited in 1959, Rockefeller's embarrassment over the shabby capital inspired him to build the mammoth marble office mall that now bears his name.

Rockefeller rarely lived at the mansion itself, but he installed a tennis court, a Picasso tapestry, and a fallout shelter.

His lieutenant governor-in-waiting, Malcolm Wilson, was a regular lodger. Attorney General Louis Lefkowitz's bedroom was where President McKinley slept the night before he was assassinated.

While the house boasts views of the Hudson and the Catskills, there was good reason to overlook the immediate surroundings. As long ago as the 1880s, the neighborhood was considered squalid.

A sneak thief once filched Al Smith's overcoat. When the Cuomos lived there full-time, a disgruntled former state janitor burglarized the place and stole several silver vases and a VCR.

That was just the element an Albany priest had in mind when he testified in 1939 against the granting of a license for a tavern virtually next door to the mansion.

His logic seemed impeccable. "A place of that kind," the priest said, "would furnish a spot for malcontents to gather."

He was referring, of course, to the tavern.

December 7, 2006

Governor Spitzer wound up spending less time in Albany than even he expected. He resigned early in 2008 after the *Times* revealed he had spent the night in a hotel in another capital, Washington, D.C., with a prostitute.

Just the Other Day . . .

"**W**atch the Times Tower" a page-one headline proclaimed in the December 31, 1907, edition of the *New York Times*. At midnight, for the first time, a lighted ball would be lowered from a seventy-foot flagpole atop the tower in Times Square to herald the New Year.

What a year 1908 turned out to be. And what a century it's been since then—in some ways that New Yorkers presciently envisioned and in others that they never could have imagined, including the fact that the ceremonial ball would still be dropped from the old Times Tower a hundred years later.

A *Times* headline forecast that "Many May Fly in 1908." And, indeed, by the end of the year, Wilbur Wright did. He would again over New York less than two years later.

H. G. Wells even published a novel in which New York was the target of a devastating enemy air attack.

The *New York World* predicted that by 2008 the nation's population would surpass 472 million—it's actually a little more than 300 million today—and that electrical power would be generated by undulating ocean tides. A Rockefeller Institute professor forecast that organ transplants would become commonplace. Other futurists said that before a century had elapsed, people would be communicating by mobile telephones.

In a new book, *America 1908*, Jim Rasenberger, a frequent contributor to the *Times*, recounts what the city was like a century ago.

Police issued a New Year's Eve ban on ticklers—those tiny feather dusters that randy men and boys wielded to titillate a woman's exposed flesh—to the extent that their flesh was exposed in 1908, and in winter no less.

So many New York women celebrated the New Year by indulging in cigarettes that the state legislature would ban women from smoking in public.

Another romantic new law didn't specify a particular form of ceremony but required couples to obtain marriage licenses.

And readers who think they remember the *Times* as the Old Gray Lady might want to recall some of the fairytale yarns that made the front pages on New Year's Eve 1908.

Like the one about the Yale baseball team captain who chivalrously decided to marry a woman whom he was rudely introduced to on the golf course when her errant ball bopped him on the head.

Or the sentimental Bronx woman who was so bereft at not being able to find a photograph of herself with her late husband that she arranged for him to be disinterred.

And that was *before* New Year's Eve.

That night, while couples embraced in Times Square, at Broadway and 34th Street a Frenchman dropped to his knees and proposed to a woman described by the *Times* as "rather pretty." She hit him on the head with her handbag. He slapped her face.

Enrico Caruso, the great tenor, celebrated at the new Plaza hotel but apparently resisted entreaties to sing. "I sing, I sing," he insisted, "but I sing later."

In a Queens saloon, there was no later for a forty-year-old man who delivered a farewell toast to 1907. "Goodbye to the old," he said. "Success to the new." Then he dropped dead.

In 1908, Harry Thaw, claiming to suffer from a distinct form of jealously diagnosed as "American dementia," would go on trial again for the love-triangle murder of Stanford White, the architect, at Madison Square Garden.

A psychologist would coin the term *adolescence* to formally distinguish children from adults.

Israel Zangwill's play *The Melting Pot* would be performed—cementing the metaphor one year after a record number of immigrants poured through Ellis Island.

And Fred Merkle, a hapless nineteen-year-old first-baseman making his debut with the New York Giants, cost the team a crucial game by slamming a line drive into center field of the Polo Grounds but neglecting to touch second base—an oversight that the *Times* denounced as an act of "censurable stupidity" and that helped immortalize the journalist Franklin P. Adams's "Tinker to Evers to Chance" ode to the double play.

New Yorkers devoured *The Fantastic Adventures of Nemo*, a comic strip starring a young precursor of Walter Mitty, whose amazing exploits every week turned out to be just a dream.

But 1908 was a time to dream. Frederick Cook, a Brooklyn doctor, embarked on a quixotic mission to the North Pole.

Coupling scientific and self-promotion, the *Times* co-sponsored an audacious 20,000-mile New York–to-Paris automobile race. It ended unceremoniously when the battered winning vehicle received a summons in the French capital for lacking a working headlight. Still, Rasenberger wrote, the race "helped ensure that automobiles would always be something more than mere machines."

From the beginning, the *Times* was ambivalent about those machines, describing them as "death-dealing agents of destruction." But the alternative was worse. Horses were still depositing an estimated 2.6 million pounds of manure each year on New York's streets.

As 1908 began, the Times Tower was the second-tallest skyscraper in New York City—just as the new *Times* headquarters on Eighth Avenue, including its ornamental mast, is tied for second place with the Chrysler Building today.

Less than two decades earlier, the tallest manmade structure in Manhattan was the steeple of Trinity Church. And already, the *Times* was warning, "Will this upward trend eventually make the city a metropolis of cliff dwellers, each looking down into a sunless canyon?"

New Yorkers of 1908 could hardly have visualized the answer, much less how much their successors would pay for the privilege.

December 27, 2007

Tusk, Tusk

You wouldn't know it from Election Day, but New York is rich in Republican history.

In fact, after analyzing the election results, you might even say that New York Republicans *are* history. These days, their best days might be behind them.

For the first time since 1942, the Democrats will hold every statewide federal and state elective office in New York. Eliot Spitzer was elected governor by the biggest margin in the state's history. He carried all but one county. Even Comptroller Alan Hevesi, accused by a state ethics commission of illegally using a state driver to chauffeur his ailing wife, was returned to office in a landslide.

Hillary Rodham Clinton's reelection margin was about the third-highest in any U.S. Senate race in New York.

And when voters were asked whether she would make a good president, 62 percent said yes. That compares with 46 percent who said the same about Rudy Giuliani and a pathetic 13 percent who agreed that outgoing governor George Pataki would.

Just before the election, the Republicans rejected New York City as the site of their 2008 national convention. Instead, they chose Minneapolis, where—listen up, Rudy—in 1892 the GOP nominated a New Yorker for vice president.

Two years ago, holding their national convention in New York for the first time, Republicans rediscovered their roots.

Republican shrines in the city include Grant's Tomb; the reconstructed birthplace of Theodore Roosevelt; Cooper Union, where Lincoln's speech propelled him toward the presidency; and statues of Horace Greeley, who christened the Republican Party in his *New York Tribune* in 1854.

A gaggle of New York Republicans stand guard in Madison Square Park, named for James Madison, a founder of the Democratic Party. There's President Chester Arthur and also Senator Roscoe Conkling— not far from where Conkling was rescued from the Great Blizzard of 1888, though he died five weeks later. Another senator, William H. Seward, may be resting on the shoulders of a giant; his relatively small head sits atop what was supposedly a sculpture of Lincoln. Legend has it that Lincoln was drafted into a supporting role when fundraising for Seward's monument fell short.

An unconventional Republican tour might include the home of Samuel J. Tilden, the Al Gore of his day. Tilden won a majority in the 1876 presidential election but lost the electoral vote. Or the building on Liberty Street, where the oil magnate Harry Sinclair hatched the Teapot Dome deals that scarred the Harding administration.

There's Central Park, where a bogus story about an escape from the zoo inspired the GOP's elephant symbol. And 812 Fifth Avenue, where Governor Nelson Rockefeller and Richard Nixon negotiated their compact in 1960 that cleared the way for Nixon's candidacy.

There's not much, except the state thruway, to memorialize Rockefeller's Republican predecessor Thomas E. Dewey, except for the enduring words of Washington wit Alice Roosevelt Longworth. In 1948, after Dewey's second defeat for president, she confided, "We should have known he couldn't win—a *soufflé* never rises twice."

Any pilgrimage to Republican shrines in New York City would be incomplete without a visit to Aziz Osmani's spice bazaar in Midtown Manhattan.

He and his cousin, both Bangladeshi immigrants, own Kalustyan's, the Middle Eastern and Indian food market at 123 Lexington Avenue. It's the only building still standing in New York City where a president of the United States—a Republican, no less—was sworn in. (George Washington, of course, was inaugurated in the city, but at the original Federal Hall, which was demolished in 1812.) In 1881, Vice President Chester A. Arthur took the oath at his home, which now houses Kalustyan's, after President James Garfield was assassinated.

This seems like a particularly appropriate time to recognize Republican symbolism of the past. It's too soon to play "The Party's Over," but in New York it's barely on life support. As Ned Regan, a former Republican state comptroller, told me on Election Night, it's comatose, but it's not dead.

November 9, 2006

For the Record

Kiss another urban legend goodbye. Now say hello to an even better one.

This one's about a nineteenth-century celebrity, Annie Moore. On January 1, 1892, the fifteen-year-old from County Cork, Ireland, was hustled ahead of a burly German and other passengers from the steamship *Nevada* by her two younger brothers. An Irish longshoreman shouted, "Ladies first," and so she became the first of 12 million immigrants who would pass through Ellis Island. The Superintendent of Immigration presented her with a $10 gold piece.

Annie Moore is memorialized by bronze statues in New York harbor and Ireland. Her arrival is recalled in story and song.

But what happened next?

According to the version that's been recounted for decades, she went west with her family to fulfill the American dream. She eventually reached Texas. She married a descendant of the Irish liberator Daniel O'Connell. Then she died, accidentally, under the wheels of a streetcar at the age of forty-six.

Turns out, though, that history embraced the wrong Annie Moore.

"It's a classic 'go-west-young-woman' tale riddled with tragedy," Megan Smolenyak, a professional genealogist, told me. "If only it were true."

The saga of the immigrant Irish girl who went west became so commonly accepted that even descendants of the Annie Moore who died in Texas came to believe it. Over the years, several of them were invited to participate at ceremonies on Ellis Island and in Ireland.

Megan Smolenyak became interested in Annie Moore while researching a documentary film on immigration. She discovered that the Annie who died near Fort Worth in 1923 was not an immigrant at all but was apparently born in Illinois.

"I realized it was the wrong Annie," she recalls.

Then what happened to the Ellis Island Annie?

It took some genealogical detective work to find out.

Smolenyak's search was reinvigorated after she visited the National Constitution Center in Philadelphia. Staring her in the face was a 1910 photograph of the Texas Annie. Smolenyak posted a challenge on her blog for information about the immigrant Annie Moore. She offered a $1,000 reward. She also mentioned her quest to Brian Andersson, New York City's commissioner of records.

"With the power of the Internet and a handful of history geeks, we cracked this baby in six weeks," she says. "Brian found this one document, and we knew we had the right family. We had the smoking gun."

What Commissioner Andersson found was the naturalization certificate belonging to Annie's brother Phillip, who arrived with her on the steamship *Nevada*. He was also listed in the 1930 census with a daughter, Anna. They found Anna in the Social Security death index. That identification led to her son, who is Annie Moore's great-nephew.

Smolenyak recalls, "As soon as I said, 'Annie Moore,' he knew instantly— 'That's us.' They had been overlooked, but they had sort of resigned themselves. They're very happy to be found."

And here's what really happened.

The Annie Moore who arrived in steerage and inaugurated Ellis Island initially joined her parents in a tenement on Monroe Street in Manhattan. She married an engineer and salesman at the Fulton Fish Market, the son of a German-born baker. They had eleven children. Five survived to adulthood. Three would have children of their own.

She endured the classic hardscrabble immigrant struggle—living all her life on the Lower East Side—and died of heart failure in 1924, at the age of forty-seven, in a tenement on Cherry Street. It was a few blocks from where George Washington lived as president. It's now the site of a housing project.

She's buried with six of her eleven children, alongside the famous and forgotten, in an unmarked grave in Calvary Cemetery in Queens. Her grave is flanked by markers for a Maxwell and a Jimenez.

Commissioner Andersson and Annie's great-niece recently donated their shares of the reward for a gravestone.

"She sacrificed herself for future generations," Megan Smolenyak says.

Annie's descendants multiplied. One of her granddaughters still lived in a public housing project on the Lower East Side until her death in 2001. Many prospered. Surviving relatives include the great-nephew, who's an investment counselor in Maryland; great-granddaughters, including a college official from Phoenix; and a nine-month-old great-great-great-great-grandson in Connecticut.

They're "poster children" for immigrant America, with Irish, Jewish, Italian, and Scandinavian surnames. "It's an all-American family," Megan Smolenyak says. "Annie would have been proud."

This seems to be one of the few cases in which a punctured myth may have enhanced a legacy instead of subverting it. As one guidebook says, "Annie Moore came to America bearing little more than her dreams; she stayed to help build a country enriched by diversity."

No editing need be applied.

September 21, 2006

The Blizzard of '06

Remember the old joke about the vaudeville star who demands a magenta spotlight? The lighting guy keeps offering various other colors, but the star is never satisfied. Finally, the guy finds the right one and shines it on the stage. The star looks puzzled. He says, "*That's* magenta?"

Which brings us to New York's Blizzard of 2006. *That's* a blizzard?

You might be asking yourself, as I did, why New York's famous Blizzard of 1888 became so iconic? After all, the Blizzard of '06 officially dumped nearly a half-foot more snow on New York City—26.9 inches in all.

I explored one theory: Maybe the snow seemed deeper in 1888 because people were shorter then. In fact, they were—on average, about three inches shorter. I checked with an expert: Richard Steckel, a professor at Ohio State. Professor Steckel, who's analyzed changes in human height, told me, yes, "that would affect people's impressions of getting through deep snow."

There's another reason the snow might have looked deeper in 1888. Not only were people shorter, but so were the buildings. The tallest in Manhattan then was only about eleven stories, shorter than the spire of Trinity Church.

Of course, the differences between 1888 and 2006 aren't only about perception.

In 1888, nobody remembered a worse storm. There had been blizzards before, but none that so devastated a city newly dependent on telegraph, telephone, and electric lights.

Technology is better today—as a direct result of the '88 storm. Downed overhead wires not only isolated New York from the rest of the world by disrupting communications and power—all of the city's synchronized electric clocks stopped at 12:07 P.M.—but they also made snow removal more hazardous. That spurred a campaign to place the wires underground.

The snow also completely halted streetcars and elevated railways. Some riders were trapped for days. That helped create demand for a subway system.

Back in 1888, officials shut down the Brooklyn Bridge because they feared it might collapse. So commuters walked across the frozen East River. High winds produced mammoth drifts. More than one hundred people died.

One prominent New Yorker, Theodorus Van Wyck, wasn't one of them. He showed up at the *New York Times* offices to prove that, contrary to some published reports, he had not been frozen in a snowbank. But Roscoe Conkling, the former U.S. senator, was, and he died a month later.

Today New Yorkers measure all big snowfalls against the blizzards of '88, 1947, and 1996. And how do we measure? Believe it or not, security guards at the Central Park Zoo read the numbers off a ruler near the sea lion pool.

If the measuring still seems primitive, the cleanup is conducted with military precision. Cleanup in 2006 was a logistical triumph, the kind that not so long ago New Yorkers would have considered beyond the ken of city government. If only we had a similar playbook to, say, improve the schools.

Before you put on an "I Survived the Blizzard of 2006" t-shirt, better listen to Ken Jackson, the Columbia University professor who edited the *Encyclopedia of New York City*. I asked him to place this record-breaking storm in historical perspective. That morning, he said, he drove fifteen miles round-trip between his home in Westchester and his gym.

"No problem," he said. "This is not something that's going to be a legend."

April 12, 2006

The Melting Metaphor

Ever wonder why the melting pot metaphor was born in New York?
Even now, the New York region gains about 500 foreign immigrants every day on average. That's more than any other metropolitan area in the nation. Five hundred a day means about 160,000 a year.

Now, let's place those figures in historical perspective.

Exactly one hundred years ago, on April 17, 1907, the Ellis Island immigration station in New York harbor recorded its busiest day ever: More than 11,000 immigrants arrived.

By the end of 1907, Ellis Island would process nearly 80 percent of the 1.3 million immigrants who entered the United States that year—a record unequaled nationally until 1990.

From its Dutch beginnings in the seventeenth century, New York was distinguished among the European colonies by its diversity. Conceptually, the melting pot as a metaphor for mixing disparate cultures can be traced at least as far back as 1782, to a naturalized New Yorker from France, and later to DeWitt Clinton and Ralph Waldo Emerson.

The specific phrase, still a touchstone of America's ongoing debate over immigration, was claimed by Samuel Schulman, the rabbi of a Fifth Avenue synagogue. He coined it in a Passover sermon he delivered in 1907—just a few weeks before that record day on Ellis Island.

Later that year, one chapter in a book by the English writer Ford Madox Ford was titled "The Melting Pot"—it credited the influx of foreigners for revitalizing Britain.

And, finally, the following year, the phrase was popularized for eternity in the title of a stage play by Israel Zangwill, the London-born Zionist son of Russian Jewish immigrants, himself married to a non-Jew.

The play preached the gospel of assimilation. The protagonist was orphaned in a Russian pogrom. He lives with his uncle on Staten Island and becomes smitten with the daughter of a Russian nobleman.

In the end, love triumphs. From the rooftop of a Lower East Side settlement house, the hero pronounces America as "God's crucible" and proclaims, "What is the glory of Rome and Jerusalem where all nations and races come to worship and look back, compared with the glory of America, where all races and nations come to labor and look forward!"

The play ran on Broadway for four months in 1909. Its title endured longer.

Edna Nahshon, a professor at the Jewish Theological Seminary in Manhattan, wrote recently, "The figurative term functions as a key image in the country's self-definition."

"Unlike its major competitors—salad bowl, stew, mosaic and symphony," she writes, "the melting pot image focuses on process, not an outcome, and presents a prophetic vision that is entirely futuristic."

The title, Nathan Glazer and Daniel Patrick Moynihan wrote in *Beyond the Melting Pot*, a half-century after Zangwill's play premiered, was "seized upon as a concise evocation of a profoundly significant American fact."

"There are boundaries," Professor Glazer explained, "particularly the black versus other, which didn't prevent miscegenation, but which did limit legitimate accepted intermarriage. That is breaking down, and Zangwill would," Glazer says, "look with favor on the increasing intermarriage across ethnic, religious, and racial lines."

In 1923, on his final visit to the United States, Zangwill urged fellow Jews to unite politically to deliver a "Jewish vote" on vital issues. He delivered a jeremiad against litter in Central Park, the glut of towels in hotel rooms, and postwar restrictions on immigration.

"You shut out immigrants instead of holding out hospitable hands," he said. "And how did you get your country? You took it by force from the Indians, and your duty is to hold it in trust for humanity. You call it 'God's own country.' For God's sake, make it so."

"When I wrote *The Melting Pot* I believed America the hope of humanity," Zangwill said. "How much more terribly true that is today!"

He returned to Britain, where he died two years later.

The other day, I found Rabbi Schulman's granddaughter in Manhattan. She says some of his descendants—in the spirit of Zangwill's melting pot—intermarried.

What about Zangwill's own offspring?

His elder son, a metallurgical engineer, emigrated to Mexico, changed his name to Jorge, and married a cattle baron's granddaughter. The couple moved to El Paso, where their three daughters were raised as Catholics. They became American citizens. Jorge Zangwill embraced Americanism as a New York Yankees fan.

Today, Zangwill's descendants in the United States are a mixture of Irish, Scotch, German, Pennsylvania Dutch, Italian, Swedish, Austrian, and Filipino.

I tracked down the playwright's granddaughter Patricia Holland-Branch in Texas. She told me, "Israel Zangwill would have been proud to know that the family he helped create has become a tapestry of diverse cultures and ethnic backgrounds. They personify *The Melting Pot*."

April 12, 2007

My New York

Hail Tilden High

Al Sharpton and I don't have a great deal in common—you could argue that's probably a blessing for both of us. But we do share a defining backdrop for our wonder years growing up in Brooklyn: At different times, we each attended Samuel J. Tilden High School.

Now New York City's Department of Education has announced that Tilden—deemed unsalvageable academically and unsafe for law-abiding students—would be permanently closed. Tilden opened during the Depression and once accommodated almost 6,000 students. It will be replaced by a cluster of more intimate and, presumably, more manageable institutions.

The *Times* story pointed out that the simultaneous closing of Lafayette High School in Brooklyn probably would attract more attention. After all, its graduates include Sandy Koufax and Larry King.

Well, Tilden alumni weren't exactly slouches.

Besides Al Sharpton, they include Mets manager Willie Randolph, the labor leader Victor Gotbaum, the lawyer and former White House counsel Len Garment, the writer Murray Polner, Judge Milton Mollen, and the weightlifter Dan Lurie. Sid Gordon batted for Tilden before being recruited by the baseball Giants to play at the old Polo Grounds. Ronnie Blye played there before joining the football Giants. The humorist Sam Levenson taught Spanish at Tilden.

Jake Ehrenreich, the singer and musician whose one-man show, *A Jew Grows in Brooklyn*, opened Off-Broadway last month, not only graduated from Tilden but makes his entrance onstage wearing a Tilden sweatshirt.

I grew up on Kings Highway one block this side of the tracks, literally, from where the New Lots El rumbled by on the border of Brownsville.

We were on the cusp of the proverbial changing neighborhood, but we proudly boasted that our block was part of East Flatbush.

And I proudly attended Tilden, which really was in East Flatbush. My sister had just graduated from Tilden, where she was editor of the student newspaper. Those were the footsteps I wanted to follow.

Tilden left an indelible impression. I still remember the taste of my daily tuna on rye and chocolate doughnut in the cafeteria. My Proustian moment was inspired by chlorine, though—I can still smell the pool. And I continue to avoid combination locks, because I shiver just thinking how I nervously fumbled with mine every time I returned stark naked to the locker room.

I was mugged once on the way home from junior high school, but at Tilden I never felt unsafe. Sure, we abandoned the annual Thanksgiving football rivalry with Jefferson because there were more injuries in the stands than on the field. And someone parodied the typically sappy school song "Hail Tilden High" as "Hail, Tilden's High," though the worst I remember that title referring to was a six-pack.

I rummaged around and found my musty 1964 Tilden yearbook. We graduated on the stage of the old Loew's Kings that year. Most of the girls said they wanted to be teachers or stenographers. One boy wanted to be a roofer. Was that really the most they aspired to? Did Ilene Kleinman become a psychiatrist? Did Philip Asher become a choreographer? Mel Feldman a race car driver? Did my friend Ira Cohen become a doctor? I had a crush on Susan Gitlin, who was voted most likely to succeed. Did she? At what?

Do we even define success the same way today?

We do know how the Department of Education defines failure.

At Tilden, fewer than 44 percent of the students scheduled to graduate last June actually did so. Only half of those graduated with a Regents diploma.

In the 1930s, Tilden established the school system's first Guidance Department, to deal with what was quaintly described as juvenile delinquency then. Now it's considered one of the city's most dangerous schools.

And after eighty years, it's about to be closed.

Between performances of his play, Jake Ehrenreich and I reminisced about Tilden. "I wonder what happens," he said. "Do buildings retain any of the feelings that were there? Do they disappear into thin air? Do they stay in our collective consciousness? Where do they go?"

I can answer only for my own consciousness. I don't know where the feelings go. But even after four decades, they don't go away.

December 14, 2006

Making It

Pete Hamill's favorite walking tour of Lower Manhattan nowadays is to a spot he calls the Place of Three Shrines.

The first two shrines are the Seward Park Public Library and the Educational Alliance. The third is the imposing twelve-story building on East Broadway that housed the *Daily Forward*, the legendary Yiddish newspaper. All three shrines share a common legacy: They initiated generations of immigrants into the English language and American culture.

Even today, more people speak Yiddish in New York than anyplace else—nearly 100,000 at last count. That's more New Yorkers than speak Russian or Korean or Greek or Polish or Arabic at home. Still, starting in the 1920s, government quotas on immigration placed a stranglehold on the *Forward*'s circulation.

My friend Jerry Adler eloquently described that shrinking readership in an article he wrote for the *Daily News* in 1977. It began: "The Jewish *Daily Forward*, the only Yiddish daily left in America, turned 80—just a few years ahead of many of its readers."

Thanks to Seth Lipsky, the editor in the 1990s, and his colleagues and investors, the *Forward* was revived with a weekly English edition in addition to the Yiddish version. Presumably, most of its readers these days are a lot younger than the newspaper, which was founded 110 years ago on the Lower East Side.

Its heritage, and New York's, is celebrated in a new book of photographs edited by Alana Newhouse, the paper's culture editor. It's titled

A Living Lens, and it's being published in conjunction with a companion exhibition at the Museum of the City of New York.

Abraham Cahan, himself a newcomer from Lithuania, was the *Forward*'s editor for the first half of the twentieth century. He viewed it as a vehicle to assimilate Eastern European immigrants. Hamill sums up its credo this way: "You can live in pride and dignity, and your American children will live even better."

That goal was universal, but it was elusive back then—as it is for many immigrants today. They sometimes needed prodding to be optimistic, given the odds against them.

Take the durable nexus between poor immigrants and crime.

"It is not astonishing," New York City Police Commissioner Theodore Bingham declared a century ago, "that with a million Jews—comprising one-fourth of the population—perhaps half of the criminals should be of that race."

Commissioner Bingham was wrong. Jews perpetrated a considerable proportion of crime in those days, but probably somewhere around a fifth, rather than half. He publicly apologized.

New York was a city of profound contrasts back then, too, not unlike today.

While Ward McAllister was chronicling the social elite whom he anointed as "The Four Hundred," Jacob Riis was photographing the abject poverty that characterized how the other half, as he called it, of New York's 4 million residents lived.

On the eve of the consolidation of Greater New York, a newspaper article hailed the new metropolis as "five prosperous boroughs" with an aggregate wealth of nearly $4.5 billion and a population that propelled New York past Paris to become, after London, the second-largest city in the world.

The day before consolidation was celebrated, Juda Sielkopelowitz jumped off the roof of his Ludlow Street tenement.

A one-paragraph news account reported that he had been despondent, in poor health, and that his wife and four children were being threatened with eviction from their Lower East Side flat for back rent.

The *Forward* was never shy about reporting on the underside of the immigrant experience. It regularly published a rogues' gallery of missing husbands. It also celebrated Jewish role models: Sidney Lumet as a child star, Bess Myerson as Miss America, Jack Dempsey as himself (a Dempsey ancestor, Rachel Solomon, was Jewish—who knew?).

In the Bintel Brief, a letters-to-the-editor column that predated Dear Abby, it also offered homespun advice to greenhorns on how to survive in New York and the New World.

One twenty-five-year-old man wrote that he was distraught because his girlfriend had a dimple in her chin. He was convinced that spouses of people with dimples in their chins die prematurely. He signed his letter, "The Unhappy Fool." The editors agreed. They replied, "The tragedy is not that the girl has a dimple in her chin but that some people have a screw loose in their heads."

Another letter-writer was concerned about reconciling religion with socialism. Should he regularly recite a memorial prayer for his dead mother? Sure, the editors replied. After all, even socialists commemorate the death of Karl Marx—who, by the way, probably learned firsthand about the class struggle as the foreign correspondent for another New York newspaper.

One reader complained to the *Forward* that friends were opposed to giving women the right to vote. To which the editors replied: "Those men are tyrants because they actually want to rule the women."

The photographs in *A Living Lens* are a mirror reflecting on an earlier tide of immigrants. I wish they were annotated, though. You wonder, whatever happened to the Aranowitz family of Brooklyn, who are pictured at a golden wedding anniversary celebration? Or to the twelve-year-old math whiz Robert Strom?

The final photograph in the book is of the newspaper's current headquarters in Midtown. Its old home on East Broadway was transformed, first into a Chinese church. It's now been converted into condominiums. You can buy a 2,600-square-foot apartment there for 2.8 million.

Imagine fulfilling the dream of American home ownership at the former headquarters of a socialist newspaper—a shrine whose terra cotta façade features a bust of Karl Marx.

June 7, 2007

The Apartment

Our extended family typically celebrates Thanksgiving in our Manhattan apartment. Not this year. The fact that our niece came to live with us last spring is only one reason.

It wasn't really her fault that she used up the last bit of gas in the apartment trying to bake a *frittata*.

Or that the toilet overflowed, flooding two rooms and ruining the carpets.

Hey, these things can happen to anyone.

Still, Kate McDonald moved in, and our lives changed overnight. Imagine a combined version of *The Apartment*, with Jack Lemmon, and *You Can't Take It with You*.

She grew up in Connecticut and was just starting her career. It's not easy to find an affordable apartment in Manhattan, of course, so we invited her to stay with us . . . temporarily. She moved into our older son's former bedroom—my office.

Within a month, we were joined by her boyfriend from Italy. He stayed six weeks.

At the end of six months, she was still here.

No matter. We have two sons, so my wife was thrilled to have a girl in the house. Even when she had to traipse dripping wet from her shower to Kate's bathroom to retrieve her pumice stone—whatever that is.

It was harder on us boys.

New applications that I couldn't pronounce, much less open, would show up on my computer desktop. Other things would suddenly vanish, like my hairbrush. Or my younger son's toothbrush. When Kate misplaced the charger for her cell phone, she "borrowed" his. It was never to be found again.

One day, the toilet in Kate's bathroom overflowed, for no apparent reason. It wasn't absolutely, positively her fault. A river ran through two rooms. Both carpets had to be removed. Dehumidifiers hummed for days. The wooden flooring was destroyed. But we took it all in stride. An inconvenience. Not a catastrophe.

On the one day in six months that Kate decided to cook, the gas in our apartment building was turned off. That wasn't her fault, either. Apparently there was a leak in the basement. Unfortunately, though, Kate hadn't fully read the signs plastered on the elevator doors. There was just enough gas left to cook her *frittata* first on the stove. Then she placed the eggs in the oven and left them to bake. We were almost asphyxiated.

Now, I'm a little reluctant to admit this part, but a week later my wife decided to make dinner. She's a great cook. We eat out a lot, though. When we're home, we often order in or use the microwave. This time, cooking required a stove. It still didn't work. Only in New York could you live in an apartment for a week without knowing you had no gas.

We didn't charge Kate rent or assign her specific chores, but on rare occasion she would reluctantly walk our golden retriever, Ernie. He is, to put it charitably, frisky and friendly. The few times Kate had attempted to take him out at night, we awoke the next morning to find alarming memos that evoked the daily crisis bulletins drafted by the White House Situation Room: "Ate aluminum foil," one read. "Chewed an elderly neighbor's sweater."

Finally my wife decided that it would help build character—Kate's, not ours—if she regularly walked the dog, just once a day. She begrudgingly agreed. Two hours later, Kate called to say she had gotten her own apartment in Stuyvesant Town.

We were in Connecticut with Kate over the weekend, visiting her folks. We drove home and dropped her off at her new apartment. Half-jokingly, I asked if she would mind taking the dog overnight. Kate said she'd be delighted. Just one problem, she added apologetically. In her new apartment, she said, pets are not allowed.

November 22, 2007

A lot of people—Kate included—thought I was too hard on her. I didn't mean to be. We miss her! So did Ernie. Meanwhile, her sister, Liz, also started living with us—without incident.

The Other Summer of Sam

"**I**t was a queer, sultry summer, the summer they electrocuted the Rosenbergs," Sylvia Plath began her autobiography, *The Bell Jar.*

I was six that summer of 1953. My father took my sister and me to the corner of our block in Brooklyn to watch the funeral procession.

Unlike lots of people touched by the atom spy hysteria, I was never consumed by the case. But I still care.

Enough to have written a book about the brother, David Greenglass, whose incriminating testimony—false testimony, he admitted to me—sent his older sister and her husband to the electric chair at Sing Sing.

Enough to have sued the federal government to release the minutes of the grand jury that indicted Julius and Ethel Rosenberg.

The suit, filed by David Vladeck and the National Security Archive, argued that ordinary secrecy and privacy are subsumed by history's compelling claim.

Fifty-five years after the execution, the government delivered a surprising response to our lawsuit: Because of the case's enduring significance, the Justice Department would not object to the release of much of the testimony.

My sixth birthday was sandwiched between the Rosenbergs' execution Friday night and the funeral on Sunday. All I knew about it was that my mother's name was Ethel; a younger brother had done something horrible to his sister (I had an older sister, too); the Rosenbergs' orphaned sons were about my age.

Among the grown-ups, two compelling questions were unspoken. Less than a decade after the Holocaust, how could Jews have done this to America? And how could America have done this to Jews?

There was a broader troubling question, about how a brother could turn against his own sister. The answer was more complicated than most people were willing to admit.

David Greenglass was a machinist. He worked on the Manhattan Project, stole atomic bomb secrets for the Russians, and claims credit for having prevented nuclear war through mutual deterrence. He was released from prison in 1960 with one wish: "All I want," he said, "is to be forgotten."

He still lives in the New York area, pseudonymously. But for the dwindling few who remember him, he remains reviled. His name became a punchline.

"Few modern events," Rebecca West wrote, "have been as ugly as this involvement of brother and sister in an unnatural relationship which is the hostile twin of incest."

In *The Book of Daniel*, E. L. Doctorow transformed David Greenglass into a retired dentist of whom it was said, "The treachery of that man will haunt him for as long as he lives."

In *Crimes and Misdemeanors*, Woody Allen's character protests to Mia Farrow's that, despite all appearances, he still loves his oleaginous brother-in-law.

"I love him like a brother," Allen says dryly. "David Greenglass."

When I began writing my book, I knew it was a story about atomic espionage, about a trial for what J. Edgar Hoover called "the crime of the century." I came to learn it was also about love and betrayal, about family dysfunction.

And when I began writing, before 9/11, I never imagined that the story would resonate so profoundly in renewed challenges of reconciling national security and civil liberties, in discomfort about blind loyalty to any cause. For the first time in fifty years, Americans would again feel vulnerable to enemy attack—threatened this time by suicide bombers, rather than suicide spies.

Who knows what smoking gun, if any, is concealed in the Rosenberg grand jury testimony? Since the trial, the weight of evidence suggests more and more that Julius was guilty—not of triggering the Korean War, as the government claimed, but of the actual legal charge: conspiracy to commit espionage. And more and more, the evidence suggests that Ethel Rosenberg was much more valuable to the Soviets as a martyr than as a spy.

Shortly before he died, I interviewed William Rogers, who was the deputy attorney general when the Rosenbergs were executed. I guess, I said to him, the government got what it wanted: The Rosenbergs were indicted, convicted, and executed.

No, he replied, the goal wasn't to kill the couple. The strategy was to leverage the death sentence imposed on Ethel to wring a full confession from Julius—in hopes that Ethel's motherly instincts would trump unconditional loyalty to a noble but discredited cause.

What went wrong?

Rogers's explanation still haunts me.

"She called our bluff," he said.

June 26, 2008

David Greenglass died in 2014.

The Final Confession

A few years ago, I asked Morton Sobell an impertinent question. Sobell is the only living American defendant from the Rosenberg atomic spy trial. The reason he's the only survivor is that the other two, Julius and Ethel Rosenberg, were put to death in the electric chair at Sing Sing in 1953.

The Rosenbergs were formally charged with conspiracy to commit espionage but were accused by prosecutors and the judge of stealing a sketch and other secrets to the atomic bomb, delivering them to the Russians, and being all but responsible for the Korean War.

Sobell was Julius Rosenberg's classmate at City College. He was an electrical engineer. He was never implicated in atomic espionage, but he was charged in the conspiracy with stealing other military and industrial secrets.

He was sentenced to thirty years. He served more than eighteen. He always professed his innocence. So, a couple of years ago, after the Soviet Union imploded and communism collapsed, I tried a trick question: If he had been guilty of espionage, would he ever admit it?

"I can't answer that," Sobell replied.

Now I know why.

The other day, Sobell confessed to me that he spied for the Soviets. He is ninety-one and lives in the Bronx. He is ailing, but he insists his long-term memory is sound.

He told me that over the summer he reached out to his nemesis, the man whose testimony helped convict him. He also said he was working on an article (with the author Walter Schneir) that amounted to a semi-confession.

Did that mean he was, in fact, a spy?

"Yeah, yeah, yeah," Sobell replied. "Call it that. I never thought of it in those terms.

"I haven't considered myself a spy," he said. "Isn't that funny. You use that word *spy*. It has connotations."

Was Julius Rosenberg a spy?

"He was a spy, but no more than I was," Sobell replied. "He gave nothing; in the end it was nothing. The sketch was negligible, and the government lied in presenting it as the secret to the atomic bomb. They never harmed this country, because what they transmitted was wrong."

Sobell, like the Rosenbergs, was a communist. He was a true believer when a rose-colored view of Russia idealized communism as a welcome antidote to capitalism—which, after all, had failed many Americans during the Depression—and to anti-Semitism, which was prevalent even in cosmopolitan places like New York but was supposedly banned in Russia.

"Now I know it was an illusion," Sobell says. "I was taken in."

So, it turns out, were all those supporters who believed he was innocent.

Sobell maintained that he was merely helping a wartime ally, that the only secrets he passed involved anti-aircraft radar and other defense mechanisms—"not stuff," he said, "that could be used to attack our country." (No matter that the technology may have been used against American combat planes in Korea and Vietnam.)

The same day I called Morton Sobell, the government released most of the Rosenberg grand jury minutes in response to a lawsuit by the National Security Archive, historians, and journalists.

Coupled with Sobell's belated confession, the testimony suggests that Julius Rosenberg was, indeed, guilty of being a spy, that Ethel was framed so the government could squeeze Julius to publicly reveal what investigators already knew about his compatriots, and that the Russians had effectively penetrated America's porous military-industrial complex.

"I remember that when I first came there," said one scientist who worked on the weapon at Los Alamos, "they told me that only certain people were supposed to know that there was an atom bomb being built, and I found out after a short time that with the exception of the common laborers and the MP's on the place, everybody else seemed to know it."

Among those who knew was David Greenglass, an Army machinist who was recruited as a spy by his brother-in-law, Julius Rosenberg.

Greenglass's false testimony sent his sister, Ethel Rosenberg, to the electric chair.

In the grand jury transcripts, David's wife, Ruth, testified that the Greenglasses were mortified when a courier, Harry Gold, gave them $500 for atomic secrets.

"When we saw the money," she said, "we realized it was no longer on a scientific plane, and we were being paid to do a job, and my husband and I felt degraded. But there was nothing we could do—we couldn't chase Gold, because we didn't know where he was going, and we kept the money."

Back then, fear was palpable on both sides—that the Russians would bomb New York, that Congress was preparing to place American communists in concentration camps. Prosecutors badgered suspects. Witnesses stonewalled. One grand juror demanded: "Ask her whether she is in favor of Russia having the atomic bomb, so that they can drop it on us," and added: "You don't deserve to be an American."

The Rosenberg case had few heroes.

"As long as I live," Morton Sobell once wrote, "I will do my best to see that this damning legacy of the cold war remains alive."

With his belated confession, he has succeeded.

September 12, 2008

Taking the Boy Out of Brooklyn

There's a good reason roosters are illegal in New York City.

You can keep female chickens—they're called hens—as pets, but not the male variety. The Health Department says the main reason is their aggressive behavior. But, hey, what about pit bulls?

I think I've discovered the real reason: Roosters would keep city dwellers awake.

Just ask Arline Bronzaft. She's a former City University professor of psychology, lives in Manhattan, and is a researcher with the city's Council on the Environment on the health effect of noise.

Not once but twice, she's testified as an expert witness on behalf of people complaining that roosters were driving them crazy.

And that was in California.

In the country.

"Roosters," Dr. Bronzaft says, "can be a problem."

All right, maybe you're wondering why they've become a problem for the *Times*'s urban affairs correspondent. It's gotten personal. Someone once defined news as something that happens to an editor or, worse yet, to an editor's spouse. Even worse, to a reporter. I spent several weekends in the country this summer, and the roosters were insufferable.

They don't just proclaim the dawn. That would be annoying enough. They keep crowing all day.

Let's face it. New York has never been a haven of serenity. This city has no silent majority. A hundred and sixty years ago, about the same time that Walt Whitman was rhapsodizing about the sounds of the city, Edgar Allan

Poe fled Manhattan to escape the noise. He found temporary refuge in the Bronx, where the relatively melodious clanging of church bells inspired him to write a poem.

In the 1930s, Mayor La Guardia—his vocal chords could overpower a loudspeaker—campaigned against horn honking. In the 1970s, people protested car alarms and the supersonic *Concorde*. New York enacted the nation's first municipal noise code—a new one takes effect next July. We even complained about ice-cream truck jingles. Just the other day, Columbia University researchers concluded that riding the subway for just thirty minutes a day can cause permanent hearing loss.

Now, I'm pretty much a live-and-let-live kind of guy, so I wouldn't think of encroaching on a rooster's right to crow. But, necessity being the mother of invention, I contrived the perfect solution.

In the city, some people blot out the street noise with the so-called white noise of a sleep machine. Well, why not turn adversity into an asset? Why not invent a city-that-never-sleeps machine for New Yorkers to take to the country?

Instead of so-called white noise, or babbling brooks, or a rhythmic surf, or a heartbeat, this sleep machine would incorporate the sounds you miss when you leave New York: piercing car alarms, horn honking, yelping sirens, grinding garbage trucks, the insistent beeping of vehicles going in reverse, the occasional manhole explosion, a gushing ruptured water main, and, depending on whether you get the X-rated model, an epithet-laced street brawl.

I forget exactly when I first got this idea, but sometime later I remember going to see the film version of *Midnight in the Garden of Good and Evil*. John Cusack, playing a New York journalist, can't doze off in sleepy Savannah without playing a tape recording of urban neighborhood noise.

The other day, I called the Marpac Corporation in North Carolina, which has been making sound conditioners and white noise generators for nearly a half-century. I suggested the company market a city-that-never-sleeps machine. Dave Tyson, the president, was cordial . . . and a bit skeptical. But he admitted that he uses a sleep machine himself and falls asleep to the sound of an artificial waterfall.

"I use a sound conditioner every night," he told me.

I asked him why.

"Because," he replied, "where I live is too quiet."

By the way, I called New York's Health Department to confirm why roosters are illegal in the city. Too aggressive is just one reason. The other? Too noisy.

October 10, 2006

Something to Crow About

Last year, you may have heard me complaining about the roosters. I'm the *Times*'s Brooklyn-born urban affairs correspondent. But in the summer I try to spend a couple of days a week away from the city to complete outside writing assignments that are inevitably overdue. I'm staying at a friend's house in northern Westchester. It's hardly a desert island. And I'm pretty adaptable. Really not a whiner. But it's remote enough from urban America to pose challenges I don't ordinarily experience in Manhattan.

Like the roosters. Last year, they woke me, predictably, at dawn. What I didn't know is that roosters don't just herald the sunrise. If they're so inclined, they'll crow all day. And shutting the windows wasn't an option, since the air conditioning wasn't working.

Even a Luddite like me instinctively knew what was wrong with the air conditioner. A succession of repairmen politely confirmed that the compressor had to be replaced. It's always the compressor. Whatever a compressor is.

This year, the air conditioner works. The windows are closed during the day. The roosters can crow all they want.

But the other morning, I was awaked by knocking on the door. At 6:00 A.M. Hesitantly, I got up to answer it. No one was there. The knocking persisted, though. After a few minutes, I finally identified the source: It was a woodpecker, or some little bird with a beak that I'm guessing was a woodpecker.

As long as I was already awake, I drove two miles to the nearest store to buy a newspaper. On the way back, I got a flat tire. I managed to get to a gas station, which was out of spares, but I ordered a new one. Three hours and $200 later, I was back at my laptop.

That's when I heard the dripping.

After scouting the uninhabited interior of the house, I discovered the closest I would come to Walden Pond—on the kitchen floor. The air conditioner again. Not the compressor, though. This time, condensation leaking from pipes in the attic.

The next night, an alarm clock began beeping. I never set the alarm in the city, but here someone must have been afraid of missing a train—the station's a twenty-minute drive. I fumbled with the alarm until I managed to defuse it. Ten minutes later, it began beeping again. I must have pressed Snooze instead of Stop.

The next afternoon, it rained. No big deal. I was working inside anyway. But it poured enough to disrupt the electricity. For five hours. For the first two of those hours, I watched the power drain out of my laptop. With no computer, and no Internet, and no light even to read by and the prospects dim for speedy repairs, I went to bed.

The other day, the telephone went dead. The computer still worked, so I went online to report the problem to Verizon. They asked for a telephone contact. I had two: One was the landline that wasn't working. The other was my AT&T cell phone, which is inoperable in isolated swaths of northern Westchester, including this one.

When I typed "Verizon repairs online," I was also referred to another website. This one said the phone company falls behind the out-of-service standard 50 percent of the time in northern Westchester. No place in New York state with as many telephones has a worse record.

So I e-mailed my wife in Manhattan. She called the company and promptly e-mailed me their response. Service, they promised, would be restored by Thursday. This was Tuesday.

I decided to turn adversity into an asset. At 9:00 P.M., I fell asleep.

At ten, my son called to say the telephone was fixed.

I had opened the window to cleanse my citified lungs with the fresh night air—which meant the incessant cackling of crickets and tree frogs also wafted into my bedroom.

Tossing and turning, I remembered that Thoreau kept a notebook under his pillow to jot down inspirational thoughts in the dark at times like these.

I did the next best thing. I returned to my laptop and Googled "Thoreau," hoping for some inspirational aphorism—or, by that point, at least some solace.

I didn't find any.

"Men have become the tools of their tools," Thoreau wrote.

Thanks, Hank.

No wonder some ascetic writers like Ted Kaczynski, the Unabomber, could be so prolific, but that others who depended more on modern conveniences, like J. D. Salinger, stopped writing altogether. (Not that I equate myself with either.)

Still seeking inspiration, I stumbled across a quote from Woody Allen. It seemed more appropriate to my annual brush with nature, my envious but vain attempt to emulate *Times* editorial writer Verlyn Klinkenborg, who revels in the rural life.

"Not only is there no God," Woody Allen said, "but try getting a plumber on weekends."

August 16, 2007

Please Don't Stop the Presses

Not long after I was hired by the *New York Times*, friends would ask how working here compared with my earlier stint at the New York *Daily News*. The answer was easy. One vivid contrast had been poignantly brought home to me years earlier. I could sum it up in three words.

Before working for the *News*, I spent a summer vacation from college as a copy boy for the *Times*. I worked nights, assigned to the bullpen, where the top editors oversaw production of the next day's newspaper.

One evening, moments after the first edition of the paper had gone to press, a clerk raced over waving a wire-service bulletin announcing that a crippling nationwide airline strike had just been settled.

In one seamless move, the new editor, Lew Jordan, rose from his chair and decisively reached for the direct phone line on his desk. Like an unflappable battlefield commander, he ordered—you guessed it—"Stop the presses."

I stood frozen, dumbstruck. Sure, I had read that phrase in books. I had heard it dozens of times in movies. But real people really saying, "Stop the presses," and meaning it?

To a college sophomore relegated to grunt work filling glue pots and getting coffee for grumpy copy editors who squirted tobacco juice at spittoons, those three words resonated as validation that my romantic visions about journalism might someday be redeemed.

I heard those words spoken again only once, several years later, when I was working at the *News*. The scene unfolded much the same way as it had a few summers before at the *Times*. A news clerk bolted into the newsroom, brandishing a wire-service bulletin, and shrieked, "Stop the presses! Stop the presses!" But this time, the editor on duty lazily looked up from his desk. He slowly shifted his gaze from the *Daily Racing Form* to the agitated young man hovering over him. "You jerk," the editor replied. "They haven't started yet."

That reflection on nearly forty years in New York journalism—forty years in which I never had the opportunity to say, "Stop the presses"—was prompted by two current events.

The *Times* is moving from our landmark building on West 43rd Street to a modern new headquarters a few blocks away. A trove of memorabilia is being auctioned off to benefit a college scholarship fund.

Also, recently I've been blessed with an award from the Silurians, a society of veteran journalists, in honor of Peter Kihss, a legendary *Times* reporter.

Peter was a friend and a mentor. When I started as a novice at the *News* covering those Sunday morning interview programs, he would sit me down afterward on a park bench and conduct a personal tutorial on the city budget and other arcana—notwithstanding the fact that we worked for rival publications.

When I finally came to the *Times*, he had already retired, but I was honored to be assigned his desk.

Peter was among the last *Times* reporters to still use a typewriter.

In newspaper city rooms, the clatter of typewriters was giving way to the tap of computers, which imposed what seemed like a disorienting silence. To compensate, the keyboards at the *News* were outfitted to emit a beep when a key was struck. The beeping was quickly disconnected, though, because the newsroom evoked the chirping of an overstocked aviary.

During my tenure there, a reporter hurled a typewriter at an editor; an office romance not only began at work but was consummated there; and an inexperienced switchboard operator inadvertently connected an editor's wife with his mistress.

Stranded couples were married in the newsroom. Criminals surrendered there, although the *News*'s experience with people giving themselves up was spotty. I remember on one slow Sunday a conscience-stricken fugitive showed up to turn himself in. Nobody wanted him.

In 1977, when the big blackout struck, *Superman* was being filmed at the *Daily News* building on East 42nd Street. Propitiously, the newsroom was bathed in generator-powered klieg lights. That made it even more difficult than usual to distinguish between fantasy and reality.

When the director of the film introduced himself to Mike O'Neill, the paper's editor, he was appreciative for the lights but unfazed by the stars. "I've got a lot of actors pretending to be journalists working for me, too," he said.

There was something surreal, also, about this week's auction of *Times* ephemera. It was held in the ground-floor mail room, not far from where the thundering presses used to spew out hundreds of thousands of newspapers every day before dawn. Technology enabled us to move to more efficient printing plants years ago. Given the potential of the Internet, it's quite possible that someday there will be no presses left to stop.

I guess that's why, with all the great photographs and other *tchotchkes* being auctioned off, what caught my eye was a well-known rectangular sheet of blue metal punctuated by buttons and lights. I'm not exactly sure what it is. Nor whether it really matters.

The *Times* scholarship fund is $200 richer for my discovery.

And me? All I know is that now I can stand up at my desk, summon up decades of remarkable memories, push that big red button on the blue metal plate, and shout to myself, "Stop the presses!"

May 17, 2007

An Affair of the Heart

I never wanted to die like Dr. Zhivago, at least not the way he did in my play-it-again-Sam memory of a middle-aged man with a neglected heart condition who dashes off a crowded bus and collapses, surrounded by strangers.

Which brings us to my wife's chest pains. And a morality tale that drove home the stark disconnect between the care the prudent medical professionals routinely recommend and what some insurance companies—apparently mine, anyway—seem willing, at least at first glance, to reimburse. This is not about a $15 co-pay.

We're talking expenses that might make the average person think twice before hightailing it to a hospital for potentially lifesaving emergency care.

Dr. Zhivago succumbed to what the American Heart Association calls "the movie heart attack." In contrast, "most heart attacks start slowly, with mild pain or discomfort," the association says, adding, "Often people affected aren't sure what's wrong and wait too long before getting help."

So when my wife called me at work to say she felt an inexplicable heaviness in her chest and had for days, I told her to call our internist immediately.

Our internist is wise and not one to panic. "Sit tight" is his typical, and usually effectual, prescription for garden-variety aches and pains. But when he heard of my wife's symptoms, knowing that her father had a history of angina, he could not have been clearer: "Go, go, go to the emergency room!"

She walked the few blocks to New York–Presbyterian on Manhattan's

East Side (the heart association recommends calling 911), arrived around noon, and received prompt and compassionate care.

She was tethered to heart monitors. Intravenous tubes were inserted. Tests were conducted. A number of potential sources for the pressure on her chest were ruled out, but still, nothing was ruled in. When a dose of nitroglycerine temporarily relieved the pain, our internist, Harvey Klein, and an attending cardiologist, Allison Spatz, decided that indigestion, which produces some of the same symptoms as heart attacks, was probably not the cause. They recommended—ordered, is more like it—that she be admitted overnight (it took until 11:30 P.M. to find a bed) so she could be observed and undergo stress tests the next day.

No food was offered to her in the emergency room (an elderly patient who was offered food was wailing about the dry string beans and mashed potatoes). So around 9:00 P.M. I went out to a pizzeria and got her some ravioli.

Later that night, I dutifully followed the instructions on my insurance ID card and called Empire Blue Cross and Blue Shield to say that my wife had been admitted. An operator efficiently took the information, assigned a case number, and cheerfully wished my wife well.

She was released around 6:00 the next evening and urged to take still more tests, including an echocardiogram and a heart scan, since the others had been inconclusive and the possibility remained that leaky valves or other heart-related defects had caused the pain.

Just three days later, we received a letter from Empire thanking us for our "medical service authorization request." It was denied. The stated reason: "Not medically necessary." The letter, signed by a doctor, elaborated that "using evidence-based criteria" the company was "unable to approve the requested coverage for acute inpatient hospital stay for evaluation of chest pain." The letter continued:

> Information received indicates stable vital signs, negative cardiac enzymes and that patient was discharged to home the next day after a negative stress test. There is no indication of abnormal EKG, previous history of unstable angina, or heart attack. As such, the evaluation of this patient, including stress test, could have occurred in a setting other than acute inpatient.

The letter added, helpfully, "Please be aware that if you proceed with this service, all medical charges will be the member's responsibility." We are appealing that decision.

It is possible, of course, that the letter was a mistake. "The standard for chest pains is very clear," said Dr. Michael A. Stocker, Empire's president and chief executive. "If a layperson thinks it's an emergency, it qualifies for payment." Not necessarily for overnight hospitalization, he said.

A week later, the hospital bill arrived: $4,949.51. That was followed by more bills: $500 from the cardiologist; $900 from a different internist; $1,308 from the hospital for additional tests ordered by the internist; $1,718 for more tests. Forget the ravioli, the gift shop purchases, and other bills that we're still getting for ancillary and miscellaneous expenses. They seem too petty to whine about.

Suffice it to say, following our doctor's advice, going to the hospital, and undergoing some, not all, of the recommended tests have cost $9,375.51 so far. Even if Empire decides that these and all the other expenses— except the overnight stay—are "reasonable and necessary" and decides to reimburse us for 80 percent of them, following our doctor's advice will still have cost us more than $4,400. Talk about chest pains.

Unlike about one in three Americans, we are lucky enough to have private health insurance, but it's not free. In addition to whatever my employer pays, I "contributed" about $4,200 in premiums last year, not counting dental, vision, or long-term-care coverage. And granted that I am form-challenged, most of the mail we get from various insurance companies is a printed list of coded, arcane, incomprehensible explanations of why they are denying reimbursement for one service or another.

But this experience raises an even more fundamental question. What happens the next time my wife has chest pains? Or I do? Or any of the people to whom we spilled our guts about this episode in sheer outrage? Will they weigh their response or their treatment too carefully because, as the insurance company seemed to suggest, this might be only their first episode of unstable angina or a heart attack? How sanguine would any of us be about following the American Heart Association's warning not to wait longer than five minutes before calling 911 and getting to a hospital?

April 10, 2005

Thankfully, Empire reversed itself after an editor correctly insisted that I call the company for comment. I couldn't help feeling that working for the *Times* and being able to reach Empire's president personally had something to do with the decision. What would have happened to anyone else?

Next

New Yorkers marry late. Not late at night, necessarily. Late in life. Later and later.

Census results just released for 2006 reveal that the median age at which men marry for the first time in New York State is 29.4—older than in every other state but three. For women, it's at 27.7 years old, so late that in the rankings of when women marry, New York is tied with Massachusetts for first place, or last place, depending on your point of view.

That factoid struck me for two reasons. First, it's just the sort of demographic change I cover as the *Times*'s urban affairs correspondent. The second reason is that my older son, Michael, got married last weekend. He and his bride may skew the next round of marrying age averages.

Mike is twenty-five. Sophie's twenty-four.

That he was early to wed should come as no surprise. For all his independence, for all his wanderlust, his very first word was *up*. As in, carry me.

But his watchword was always *next*. I remember the first time he told us he wanted to get married and move out. He was five.

He escaped from his crib long before he should have been able to climb or crawl. Someone suggested we install razor wire, but we opted for a more humane solution: We paid him to stay in his room.

It worked. Too well. That marked the beginning of a long tradition of incentive-based motivation. We paid him to learn how to bike ride. To ice skate. To read a book.

But the investment was worth it. Next month, Mike starts a new job. He will make more money than I do. He's promised to put my wife and me in a good home.

Sooner, I hope, than later.

The wedding last weekend evoked other stories, too.

There was the time he thought it was cute to place a toilet plunger on his head. Until we told him what a toilet plunger was.

For a drama class ten years ago, he wrote a play that encapsulated his life as a young New Yorker. There was the Mike character:

> Complaining about the dog hairs lodged on his backpack; Screaming at his younger brother for one reason or another; Commiserating with a classmate on the phone, quote: "How the hell am I supposed to know why hydrogen molecules bond with sulfur molecules"; And beseeching his mother to buy him a leather desk chair.

Mike never took himself too seriously, though. Consider this dialogue he wrote for himself in that school play: "I know it's expensive, but it was really cool and it was from Ralph Lauren. It's the kind of chair I'll keep forever. I'll even take it to college."

To which his mother replies, according to Mike's script: "Oh sweetheart, sure! A thousand-dollar leather chair. Whatever you want."

Right!

In junior high, he was assigned a social studies paper. He could write about any country in Africa. Mike chose Chad. Why Chad? I asked. His explanation was quintessential Mike: He didn't want to have to type Mozambique over and over again.

The problem was, nothing ever happened in Chad. So Mike and I deftly crafted what seemed like a perfectly ambiguous first paragraph: "Chad is a metaphor for a nation of contradictions." It sounded really profound at the time. His mother made us dumb it down.

His brother remembers that we should have known when Mike was still in high school that he had the makings of a great lawyer. After exhaustive research, he presented his parents with a ten-page brief in which he convincingly argued the merits of buying a radar detector. He lost that case.

From the beginning, life with Mike has always been an adventure.

At the wedding, he and Sophie said: "We only hope to one day give our children all that we have been given."

Kind of makes it all worth it.

September 13, 2007

Mike and Sophie celebrated their eleventh anniversary in 2018 with their twin daughters.

Seen on the Subway

Guess what I saw in the subway the other day.

It was nearly hidden on a New York City Transit public service placard exhorting riders not to leave their newspapers behind when they get off the train.

"Please put it in a trashcan," readers are reminded. After which an erudite copy editor in the Metropolitan Transportation Authority's marketing and service information department inserted a semicolon. The rest of the sentence reads: "that's good news for everyone."

A semicolon? Go ahead, ask. What's the big deal?

Forget that the newspaper being unceremoniously discarded under the subway seat in the accompanying photograph happens to be the *Times*.

Or that you might once have seen a semicolon in a transit *Poetry in Motion* poster. Those don't count. They're poems. Not pronunciamentos crafted for public consumption by committees of civil servants.

Semicolon sightings in the city are unusual because they signal something New Yorkers rarely do.

Frank McCourt, the author and former English teacher at Stuyvesant High School, describes the semicolon as the yellow traffic light of a New York sentence. In response, most New Yorkers accelerate; they don't pause to contemplate.

In literature and journalism, to say nothing of advertising, the semicolon has been largely jettisoned as a pretentious anachronism.

Especially by Americans.

We prefer shorter sentences without, as stylebooks advise, that distinct

227

division between statements that are closely related but require a sepa-
ration more prolonged than a conjunction and more emphatic than a
comma.

One response to a *Financial Times* essay on punctuation not long ago
went so far as to suggest that the semicolon was anti-American. Why?
Because it was an invitation to prolonged idleness, it "presumes that the
reader has no more immediately satisfying option than allowing the writer
to finish his thought."

"When Hemingway killed himself he put a period at the end of his
life," Kurt Vonnegut once said. "Old age is more like a semicolon."

New York City public schools are supposed to introduce semicolons
to students in the third grade. But let's be frank. Whatever your personal
feelings about them, some people don't use semicolons because they never
learned how.

One of the school system's most notorious graduates, David Berkowitz, the Son of Sam serial killer who taunted police and the press with
rambling handwritten notes, was, the columnist Jimmy Breslin wrote, the
only murderer he'd ever encountered who could wield a semicolon just
as well as a revolver. (Berkowitz, by the way, is now serving an even longer
sentence.)

The rules of grammar are routinely violated on both sides of the law.

People have lost fortunes, even been put to death, because of imprecise
punctuation involving semicolons in legal papers. Just a couple of years
ago, a court rejected a conservative group's challenge to a statute allowing
gay marriage because the operative phrases were separated incorrectly by
a semicolon instead of by the proper conjunction.

Some American writers complain that semicolons are subversively ambiguous, that they vaguely imply a connection between two statements
without having to specify what that connection is.

A New York writer scolded *The Financial Times*: "I submit to you
that we care more about New Orleans, Iraq, and what backpack our kids
need for school" than about semicolons. "What do you think we are?"
the writer asked. "Editors?"

Or linguists. Speaking of which, Louis Menand, the Harvard English
professor and *New Yorker* staff writer, pronounced the subway poster's use
of the semicolon to be "impeccable."

Lynne Truss, author of *Eats, Shoots and Leaves*, the bestselling book
about punctuation, called it a "lovely example" of proper punctuation.

Geoffrey Nunberg praised the "burgeoning of punctuational literacy
in unlikely places."

The linguist Noam Chomsky sniffed, "I suppose Bush would claim it's the effect of No Child Left Behind."

"What's next?" said Ben Yagoda of the University of Delaware. "Synecdoche"?—which means, more or less, a figure of speech.

New York City Transit's uplifting agenda notwithstanding, e-mails and text messaging may jeopardize the last vestiges of semicolons. They still survive, though, in emoticons, those graphic emblems of our grins, grimaces, and other facial expressions.

And guess what the semicolon symbolizes: It's a wink.

February 14, 2008

This podcast dominated the *Times*'s most e-mailed list of stories for nearly a month. I suspect that's because English teachers were forwarding it to their students and copy editors to one another.

Brownsville

The day I was born, two people identified as Negroes made their way onto the pages of the *New York Times*.

One was the suspect who showed up at Holy Cross Church in Times Square and walked away with $300 in poor-box collections from an open safe.

The other was Francis Turner of Harlem, who was just named the city's assistant director of community education—the highest rank ever attained by a Negro in the school system. Turner scored second on the exam for the job (just behind Hyman Sorokoff) but received preferential treatment because he was a military veteran.

Another Negro who was making news regularly and who paved the way for Barack Obama was off that day, between games for the Brooklyn Dodgers.

Jackie Robinson was just one reason for Harlem's optimism that June of 1947, the author Roi Ottley wrote in the *Times*. "Removal of the 'For Whites Only' sign from many jobs has opened new horizons to the Negro and choked off his loudest complaints," he wrote.

A decade earlier, fully 80 percent of black working women were employed as household help. In 1947, about 60 percent were. W. E. B. Du Bois was predicting that by 1965, blacks would have a fair chance to earn a decent wage, would no longer be bound by residential segregation, and would universally be able to vote.

And white Americans might eventually look past color in their own self-interest. "The fact is," Roi Ottley wrote, "Negroes do not believe the

United States can long lecture the world about democracy without doing something concrete about democracy at home. They are aware that the country's moral position is at stake."

I grew up in Brownsville, which was a misnomer. It was solidly white and almost as solidly Jewish. It was named for Charles Brown, a developer who in the late nineteenth century began marketing the largely Scottish settlement to Jewish refugees from the Lower East Side. As early as 1893, the *Brooklyn Eagle* reported: "The Jews have driven out the Scotch."

Growing up in Brownsville, I didn't know any Scots—or Negroes. Except for Neville, who lived somewhere even deeper in Brooklyn and who every few years was hired to paint our apartment. And, of course, a cleaning woman. My family was considerably more progressive than some of our neighbors, but the conversation between the parents of Woody Allen's character in *Annie Hall* comes close to capturing the liberal spirit of the times:

"You fired the cleaning woman?"
"She was stealing."
"But she's colored."
"So?"
"They're persecuted enough!"
"Who's persecuting? She stole!"
"All right—so we can afford it . . . She's a colored woman, from Harlem! She has no money! She's got a right to steal from us! After all, who is she gonna steal from if not us?"

While we lionized breakthrough Jewish achievers, we were taught a special respect for accomplished blacks: Ronnie Blye, who would play football in the 1960s for Tilden High School (where two decades earlier Francis Turner taught Phys. Ed.), and Ralph Bunche, who was polishing America's image at the UN.

Just two months before I was born, Jackie Robinson was generally well received in his debut at Ebbets Field. Arthur Daley, the *Times*'s sports columnist, quoted one veteran Dodger—conspicuously unnamed—as saying: "Having Jackie on the team is still a little strange, just like anything else that's new. We just don't know how to act with him. But he'll be accepted in time. You can be sure of that. . . . I'm for him, if he can win games. That's the only test I ask."

For all the self-congratulation after Election Day 2008 about how much progress America has made, that was sixty-one years ago—as distant as 1886 (two decades after the Civil War) was back in 1947.

Today, in my old Brownsville census block group, six of the 1,300 residents are white, which probably makes it more integrated than when I grew up there.

Barack Obama carried my old election district 378 to 0. He won New York state with 62 percent, which is more than any presidential candidate since Lyndon Johnson, who was inaugurated in 1965—the year W. E. B. Du Bois predicted that blacks would achieve the full benefits of citizenship.

Of course, people measure progress in different ways. As Bella Abzug once said, "Our struggle today is not to have a female Einstein get appointed as an assistant professor. It is for a woman *schlemiel* to get as quickly promoted as a male *schlemiel*."

Still, Election Day exit polls suggest just how much has changed over three generations: About twice as many voters in New York and elsewhere said the age of the candidate was a more important factor in their decision than his race.

November 6, 2008

Obama's New York

A few weeks ago, addressing the annual dinner honoring Al Smith, New York's legendary governor, John McCain declared, "America will always remember the boy born in an old tenement on South Street in Brooklyn."

Smith, of course, *was* born on South Street, but in Manhattan, on the Lower East Side. It was just a minor slip, barely noticed, presumably no reflection on McCain's memory. But in a small way, it suggested how far New York's political capital has been diminished and how the urban agenda that Smith championed has been largely overlooked in the 2008 presidential campaign.

Maybe that's because problems once considered exclusively urban have become commonplace well beyond the nation's cities. Maybe it's because voters in so many cities have been taken for granted, while the candidates lavish their attention on the dwindling number of swing states still up for grabs.

But in the 2008 presidential debates—including one held next door to New York City—the words *cities, urban, mass transit,* and *homelessness* were never even mentioned. *Infrastructure* came up once, in an Obama reference to Middle East oil production. He also made a passing comment about crime.

This year's elongated campaign never generated much hope that any of the candidates considered urban problems their priority—even though the frontrunners once included a former New York mayor and a senator from New York.

It's all but forgotten, but New York has produced more presidents and vice presidents—thirteen of them—than any other state.

In *The Bear Went Over the Mountain*, a charming Baedeker of presidential gravesites, Carll Tucker suggests one explanation: New York was never homogeneous. Candidates had to reconcile diverse constituencies. Being above politics was considered a liability. "New Yorkers," Tucker writes, "are trained to ceaselessly sniff for self-interest."

Perhaps it's presumptuous to claim Barack Obama as a New Yorker, but at least he lived here for a couple of years. He arrived in 1981 to attend Columbia. (He'd be the first Columbia graduate elected president; also, of some note to a city of immigrants, the first since Herbert Hoover with a parent born outside the United States.)

Obama recalls spending his first night in an alley near West 109th Street because he couldn't get into his off-campus apartment. He says he bathed the next morning alongside a homeless man at a fire hydrant. He lived with a Pakistani roommate and later moved to a walk-up in East Harlem, where many of his neighbors were Puerto Rican. He jogged three miles a day.

It was only then, Obama wrote in his memoir, "that I began to grasp the almost mathematical precision with which America's race and class problems joined; the depth, the ferocity, of resulting tribal wars; the bile that flowed freely not just out on the streets but in the stalls of Columbia's bathrooms," where racist and anti-Semitic graffiti flourished.

He worked to pay off student loans, then was hired as a community organizer by the New York Public Interest Research Group. He spent three months at City College mobilizing student volunteers, trying, as he recalled, to convince minority students "about the importance of recycling."

Eighty years earlier, on an otherwise uneventful October evening, a president of the United States from New York invited a black man to dine with him at the White House.

Blacks had dined there before, but they were servants confined to the kitchen. A few blacks had visited, too. Frederick Douglass, the escaped slave who fled to New York and rose to become a presidential elector from the state, was once invited to the White House with fellow officials from the District of Columbia by President Grover Cleveland, another New Yorker.

But Theodore Roosevelt's private White House dinner in 1901 with the educator Booker T. Washington shocked the nation and touched off a virulent political backlash—and not only in the South.

One *Times* reader—from New Jersey—wrote that whites and blacks "must reach their destinies in this country along parallel lines, let us trust, but with the lines never approaching social unity."

Another reader recalled that just the summer before, he was surprised to see Booker T. Washington dining in the men's café of Manhattan's Grand Union Hotel. The headwaiter explained: "We do not entertain all colored people, but that is a great man over there—that is Mr. Washington, who runs the college down South."

America has come a long way since then. Even since Obama's experience in New York. Teddy Roosevelt and his cousin Franklin, who was Al Smith's successor as governor, brought an urban sensitivity to the White House that few successors matched, and that Barack Obama now holds the promise to fulfill.

October 30, 2008

Even before he was inaugurated, President Obama nominated three New Yorkers—Hillary Rodham Clinton, Shaun Donovan, and Timothy Geithner—to his cabinet. He later appointed Bronx Borough President Adolfo Carrión Jr. director of a new White House Office of Urban Affairs; Thomas R. Frieden, the health commissioner, as director of the Centers for Disease Control and Prevention; Rocco Landesman, the Broadway producer, as chairman of the National Endowment for the Arts; and Judge Sonia Sotomayor to the United States Supreme Court.

Acknowledgments

Thanks to Jon Landman at the *Times* for suggesting that I write and narrate the "Only in New York" podcast and to Jim Roberts, Jane Bornemeier, Tom Bartunek, Pedro Rosado, Patrick LaForge, Sewell Chan, Lexi Mainland, Emily Rueb, and Michael Rich for making it possible every week.

I'm also grateful to Alex Ward and to my persistent agent, Andrew Blauner; to the editors at St. Martin's Press who originally published these essays; and to Fred Nachbaur and Eric Newman at Fordham University Press, who so gracially supported this edition. And special thanks to all of you for listening and reading, and to a city that keeps on giving.

ESE SELECT TITLES FROM EMPIRE STATE EDITIONS

R. Scott Hanson, *City of Gods: Religious Freedom, Immigration, and Pluralism in Flushing, Queens*. Foreword by Martin E. Marty

Mark Naison and Bob Gumbs, *Before the Fires: An Oral History of African American Life in the Bronx from the 1930s to the 1960s*

Robert Weldon Whalen, *Murder, Inc., and the Moral Life: Gangsters and Gangbusters in La Guardia's New York*

Joanne Witty and Henrik Krogius, *Brooklyn Bridge Park: A Dying Waterfront Transformed*

Sharon Egretta Sutton, *When Ivory Towers Were Black: A Story about Race in America's Cities and Universities*

Pamela Hanlon, *A Wordly Affair: New York, the United Nations, and the Story Behind Their Unlikely Bond*

Britt Haas, *Fighting Authoritarianism: American Youth Activism in the 1930s*

David J. Goodwin, *Left Bank of the Hudson: Jersey City and the Artists of 111 1st Street*. Foreword by DW Gibson

Nandini Bagchee, *Counter Institution: Activist Estates of the Lower East Side*

Carol Lamberg, *Neighborhood Success Stories: Creating and Sustaining Affordable Housing in New York*

Susan Celia Greenfield (ed.), *Sacred Shelter: Thirteen Journeys of Homelessness and Healing*

Elizabeth Macaulay-Lewis and Matthew M. McGowan (eds.), *Classical New York: Discovering Greece and Rome in Gotham*

Susan Opotow and Zachary Baron Shemtob (eds.), *New York After 9/11*

Andrew Feffer, *Bad Faith: Teachers, Liberalism, and the Origins of McCarthyism*

For a complete list, visit www.empirestateeditions.com.